Between Frederick Bue
Journey and Russell Bak
Matt Matthews' *One Th*
all its own through th
written and meticulous
son's pilgrimage into the heart of his father's story is a treat for
believers and non-believers, for anyone fascinated with WWII
and the generation that endured it, with the metes and bounds
of family and memory, with history; in short, for everyone. This
is a wonderful book.

Janet Peery, author of *The River Beyond the World*,
a National Book Award Finalist

Matt taps into my own longing to understand and connect with
my three-time war veteran father and my own need to make
sense of that war's enduring legacy . . . This is a "must read"
for all children and grandchildren of these Silent Generation
war heroes—and for families of every man and woman coming
home from a modern day war zone.

Mark W. Lenneville, Chaplain (LTC), US Army, (retired).

Written with insight, humor and grace, *One Thousand Miles*
is a window through which all fathers and sons, and all who
have ever had a father or a son, can see the other (and maybe
themselves) anew.

Barrie Miller Kirby, author of
No Such Thing as A Cherokee Princess

This is a splendid book.

David Bartlett, Professor Emeritus at Yale Divinity School
and Columbia Theological Seminary.

[An] extraordinary story of an "ordinary" American family . .
. For those of us who did not live through WWII the book is
a gentle but insistent transport. For those who did, it will be a
welcome reminder of some of the most important meanings of
the overused word "honor."

Don Belanus, Captain, Chaplain Corps, USN (retired).

[S]mart, funny, keenly observed . . . There's no epiphany here, but by following his father's footsteps during the war, Matthews comes to understand his father and his family in new ways, and we feel enlightened by having been along for the ride.

Deno Trakis, author of *Because Memory Isn't Eternal* and the novel *Messenger from Mystery*

Matt Matthews' superb *One Thousand Miles* is part history, part travelogue, part memoir—and all heart.

Deb Richardson-Moore, pastor, Triune Mercy Center, Greenville, and author of *The Weight of Mercy*, and *The Cantaloupe Thief*.

One Thousand Miles is as profoundly engaging as it is beautifully crafted. Matt Matthews writes with compassion, humor, and the wisdom to let moving events speak for themselves. The result is a richly layered narrative of love between a son and his father. For both Matthews and the reader, it ultimately becomes a meditation on what to release and what to keep forever close as we move into a future that honors the love we feel for another.

Steve Doughty, author of *The Man with Six Typewriters*; *To Walk in Integrity*; *The Way of Discernment*

Matt has written an excellent book.

Art Baiden, Major General, US Army Reserves, (retired).

One Thousand Miles
Following My Father's WWII Footsteps

by
Matt Matthews

978-1-946879-00-4

HISTORY / Military / World War II

BIOGRAPHY & AUTOBIOGRAPHY / Personal Memoirs

Books may be ordered through booksellers or by contacting:

Avenida Books www.avenidabooks.com

Printed in the United States of America

Avenida Books

A |V

Also by Matt Matthews

Fritz & Christine and Their Very Nervous Parents
a book for children and the adults who love them

Mercy Creek
winner of the South Carolina Arts Commission First Novel Prize

Matt Matthews sometimes updates a webpage at:
www.MattMatthewsCreative.com

For our sons.

Thanks—

♥ Barbara Burriss Matthews, consummate mother who prods me, even now, to wear a jacket when it's chilly outside ● Tom Hester, patron, critic, friend, *still* ● BMK who always said the right thing ● Jim Burrows, poet and purveyor of the worm's eye view, r.i.p. ● Our Scots tour guide, Martin King ● The timely hospitality of the Funke family ● Travel experts Walter and Mary Margaret Burgess ● Bill Turner for the miles ● Hu Lacquement, Col. US Army, Ret., whose insight and Battle of the Bulge library was a boon ● Betsy Teter and the inspiration and friendship of the *world changers* at the Hub City Writers Project ● The sabbatical committees and fellow saints at the amazing St. Giles Presbyterian Church ● Rebecca Bowen Roper ● Don Kirkland, The Brave ● Jill Hendricks ● Bret, Deb, Fiona, & Sodak Godfrey ● Andrew Barron ● Eddie Ricketts, bowed but not broken ● Fr. Furman Buchanan, confessor, friend ♥ *Rachel, Joseph, Benjamin, & John Mark Matthews* with whom I am blessed to share this and all journeys.

A generous grant provided by the Louisville Institute funded a sabbatical from my duties as pastor of St. Giles Presbyterian Church, Greenville, SC. Heartfelt thanks to both Institute and Church for the funds and time away for research and writing.

The first letter of the first word of the first commandment is an aleph. An aleph is silent. An aleph is the very beginning of the conversation.

—Rabbi Sandy Sasso

When my old man grinned, nobody could help but grin too.

—Ernest Hemingway, *My Old Man*

I want to carry you
And for you to carry me
The way voices are said to carry over water.

—Billy Collins, *Carry*

Contents

1 Parsing Coordinates on Hallowed Ground   13

2 Gently Back to Earth: Landfall in Liège   19

3 Blood and Guts   38

4 Midnight Is A Place   47

5 Manhood   75

6 Almost Lost in Translation   81

7 The 9:49 to Paris-Nord   89

8 Luminous Paris   100

9 Normandy   109

10 A Perfect View   122

11 Neither Sighing   130

12 Making Full Use of the Platform   145

13 A Riddle of Steel and Stone   160

14 To Think Many A Man Made A Meal of It   171

15 Bridge Over Troubled Water   179

16 If Only I'd listened to Sherlock Holmes   189

17 Going, Going, Gone   200

Selected Notes   205

1

Parsing Coordinates on Hallowed Ground

I am trying to picture my dad's face as we fan out along the top of this wooded ridge in the Ardennes. This is very near—as close as our guide will get us—to where Dad fought in the Battle of the Bulge. As a kid, I pumped my old man for war stories, but through the decades, I got only a delicate few. His happy face would go slack. He'd look away. My late father told me little about his part in the war he seldom mentioned.

I strain to imagine the wartime snow that slammed into these woods as ferociously as the Germans did in 1944, but the June breeze is too delicious for me to envision such a cruel December. Stiff from the long drive, I stretch. It feels good to walk beneath this cathedral of pine. The day is postcard perfect—sunny, warm, cheery blue skies. Our guide Martin, my three sons, and my wife stroll on cat's feet. It's just us in these woods.

Dad's image flickers in and out. His absence is like a presence to me. Even as an old man he wore a boyish, friendly expression; yet, were he here, still living, he would look ancient. Were he here, I might reach out to touch his shoulder and then pull back. I wouldn't want to disturb him. I had pestered him enough about the war over the years. He would be quiet, as I am quiet now. He would avoid my eyes.

On December 16, 1944, snow showers and low clouds made it impossible for Dad's 422nd Regiment to see the Germans. But they were there, and coming. There was no way to soften the roar of Panzer tanks and trucks crammed with volksgrenadiers as they groaned west below this ridge. The macadam roads were a disaster—narrow, bogged in mud, and often obscured by snow—but the Germans charged as quickly as conditions allowed towards St. Vith, the Belgian town nearby, and other points west. Dad had no place to hide, save for the foxholes that tourists would still be able to find sixty-seven years later. They were ghosts, this unseen enemy and their machines. They shouted in a language Dad may have recognized from the Saturday operas he listened to on the living room radio back home in Virginia. These soldiers, however, were not singing.

Distant birdsong provides the soundtrack on this early summer day. There is no crowd, no traffic, no interruptions. A few shafts of sun penetrate the high canopy of pine branches drawing golden splotches on the ground that dance with the breeze. My wife Rachel steps from the dappled, cool shade and kneels in a glowing oval of sun to admire the blue bellflowers poking through the ground cover. Our three sons walk together to the edge of the ridge. Needles pad their steps. The younger two look to their oldest brother for cues. Joseph stands silently, so they also are silent. I can hardly speak.

With trembling fingers Dad checked the strap of his helmet, cinched it tight, hunched his shoulders, held his head low, kept his rifle at the ready. He could smell the snow and the dirt and the vomit from nervous men around him. He stomped his freezing feet; their company was last on the list to get delivery of army-issue overshoes. His regiment of 3,000 had dug in only five days before, and their supplies were still catching up. It was the coldest winter in forty years. If the Germans didn't kill them—and they aimed to—living in the outdoors in the stinging cold would.

Joseph, 18-years-old, is Dad's age when Dad had gone through basic training in Oklahoma and Indiana. It crushes me to think of my first son ill-clad and suffering 4,500 miles from home in winter cold, yet, I can't stop my imagination. He is damp, blowing into his cupped hands, nearly unrecognizable in uniform, crouched like Dad waiting to kill or be killed. I blink hard, twice, and look at him gazing off at the farms below us. Benjamin and John Mark look pale and older in this filtered light, kindly ghosts of another sort. From what travails will I be unable to protect them, as my grandparents were unable to protect their two sons?

I am reduced to clichés. Dad is so close yet so far away. The sudden weight of missing him disorients me. I remember snatches of half-conversation wheedled out of him about what happened on this ground. The air smells of pine and flowers. Treetops sway beneath a dome of clear blue sky. It is quiet like a church.

Hoarse with emotion, these Americans only recently off the boats and unbloodied so far by the European War effort barked at one another. *Is this it? Where are they? Are the krauts coming or not?* Snow and clouds had blanketed this lovely tree-lined ridge turning everything a Christmas card white. There was a lot they couldn't see. So much they couldn't know. There was no chance of air support in this soup. No relief was in sight. And they had no idea how alone they were and how cut off from the rest of their division they had become. They didn't know yet that most of them were doomed.

Unless you're lost, this out-of-the-way place isn't on the way to somewhere else. Right on the border of Belgium and Germany, there are no stores, homes, or farms in this forest. Besides area teenagers who park up here to make out, the only people who visit are people with something to find, aged American vets, among them, trying to remember where they had dug in when German steel split the dawn and trees splintered and snow covered everything.

The grunts—basic riflemen like Dad—waited for orders. Lieutenants, who had trained in the strategy of battle but had never tasted it, checked their maps. They strained into binoculars pointed eastward into Germany. They checked their maps again. And again. They were waiting for orders from Colonel Descheneaux in Schlausenbach, or from higher-ups 11 miles behind them in St. Vith. Radio communications were spotty. Everyone waited for orders—except for the Germans, who had theirs. They smashed through the thinly defended lines on the Belgian-German front, lurching heavily through the farms, crossroads, and towns that American troops scrambled to defend, then abandon. This blitzkrieg could not be denied, especially in the first hours when everyone was caught off-guard, and even if ready, were so ill-provisioned and undermanned to repel for long.

Martin sidles up to me. He studiously follows my gaze. Yellow-green fields spread out below. One field is carved by a mile-long serpentine line of blonde hay coiled in tractor-sized rolls. On another field, a few spindly trees cluster around distant, weathered barns.

"We're close," he whispers.

"Am I looking towards Germany?" I ask.

He touches my shoulder and turns me around. He points. "Now you are," he says quietly. "Right down *there*."

It is close. And it is from this direction that my father and the rest of the 422nd and 423rd regiments of the 106th Division had expected the German attack. They did not know that by nightfall on the first day of battle the Germans had *almost* already surrounded them and were directing their formidable resources beyond them, *behind them*, to the west. This bulging Allied line is where the battle got its unfortunate name.

"This," Martin said, "is really close, Matthew. Your dear father stood very near this place."

I nodded.

Everyone on the ridge kept their heads low, tested their trigger fingers, swallowed hard, prayed or pleaded. They weren't allowed to smoke lest a sniper draw a bead on the lit end of a soldier's cigarette, but they could blow frost rings into the frigid air. Their squatting bodies began to freeze in place. As soldiers are wont to do before battle, some made their peace with God. Some were resigned. Some thought they were ready. All of them were freezing. All were hungry, all afraid.

This was it.

And they waited.

Private first class William P. Matthews, from Hampton, Virginia, was O-positive, Caucasian, five-nine, and 144 pounds without his pack. He parted his dirty blonde hair on the left and had a ready smile and blue eyes. He could tell a joke. He wasn't shy. Everybody called him Billy. He was twenty-years-old. In less than forty-hours he would be a prisoner of war.

I have tried to parse the coordinates from all the confusing battle maps I have studied over the years. Altitude, contours, the wide sky and the cribbed forest. Things are different on the ground. There are no pencil marks and arrows drawn on this earth. In which direction is Schlausenbach? Martin has driven us over so many curvy roads, through so many villages, that I feel a little seasick. We have come from the south, from Bastogne. Patton had got to this spot by many of the roads we have just followed. I wonder where Ihren Creek is, and the Schönberg Road. I can't hear the battle in this quiet stillness. I had thought I might. I had thought some noise of battle would linger. There is no low groan of tank engines, no pop-pop-pop of small arms fire, no cannon. Nothing. I had halfway expected some tired GI to wander up to us from the brush. "Fellas, you got a Coke? I'm dying for a swig of something sweet."

But none of the battle weary make an appearance. I can't even hear their cries, and I listen closely, cocking my head at every point of the compass. I can't smell the diesel belching from German tracked armor and the 25-ton tanks churning the narrow roads below to porridge. I can't even feel the penetrating cold, which surprises me most. I want to ask Martin if he is sure this is the place. Is Martin sure this is the place Dad stood—these warm, stately woods, this shadowed ridge, this graveyard silence?

Modern, white wind turbines stand like steeples; their elegant tri-blades circle languidly in the breeze while their solid white trunks, tapering a little wider at the bottom than the top, remind me of a narrow teepee, or the white alb of a tall priest pronouncing a solemn benediction. Besides the silted foxholes, no evidence exists that anything but beauty ever graced this gently rolling land. Two hawks ride the thermals ascending from the sun-warmed fields. The Scots pine in which we stand have no low branches and their naked trunks shoot straight up, piercing that innocent, blue sky like arrows. My family has spread out beneath the trees, each of us looking his or her own way, turning over private thoughts.

I find myself constantly looking for Dad. When I close my eyes, I don't see a man in uniform less than half my age haggard by cold and fear. I don't see a soldier at all. Instead I see a grandfather with a full mane of white hair as he sits on a wooden front porch swing, teaching two-year-old Joseph how to clap. He wore no uniform, only a contented expression and kind eyes, and a striped polo shirt.

And when I open my eyes, I see my jet-lagged family at the end of the first day of a three week trip from America. Rachel still gazes out over the fields. The boys chat. What are they thinking? When our boys look around do they see what they remember of their Pops? John Mark, who used to nap in his lap, was only two when he died a decade before. Do my boys even remember what my dad looked like?

Dad was ill equipped to say much about the emotional landscape of the war, but he did say more than once how beautiful this part of Belgium was. Quaint towns. Hills. Trees. *Real nice*, he said. *Real nice*. We are here. And he was right.

I watch the hawks twist slow circles in that wide, summer sky. The ridge between St. Vith and Schönberg is where the 168th Engineering Combat Battalion defended the St. Vith Road, the road that Dad had desperately scrambled to find. In a clearing below us, near that road, he and most of his regiment either surrendered or died. If I knew precisely where to look—if Martin could pin point the exact spot—I am certain that I will be able to see my dad before the enemy carts him off.

I'd wave. And this young stranger named Billy Matthews would wave back.

2

Gently Back to Earth
Landfall in Liège

John Mark, eleven-years-old and our youngest, was my
seatmate on the flight from Atlanta to Brussels. We fought
for control of the armrest. When I finally seized it for keeps,
I did so without guilt. I had earned it. I'd changed his diapers
when he was a child, after all. My father, who on no occasion
changed my diapers, never would have stolen anything from
me. He always put my comfort above his. But I am not my
father. John Mark fit comfortably in his seat. I filled mine like
a walrus. Night crept too slowly towards morning. The flight
was interminable. Sleep would never come.

Twain, writing about French trains, well describes air travel
some forty years before the Wright brothers lifted off the
dunes at Kitty Hawk. If you must sleep, he wrote in *Innocents
Abroad*, "[Y]ou must sit up and do it in naps, with cramped
legs and in a torturing misery that leaves you withered and
lifeless the next day." When the Apostle Paul talks about being
poured out like a libation, he's talking about the red-eye from
Damascus to Rome via Detroit.

Talking with John Mark brought my only light. Joseph and 14-year-old Benjamin, seatmates across the aisle and one row up, were too distant for talk; they weren't into chatting with their old man, anyway. Rachel, motionless as a gargoyle, had curled into a seat next to John Mark. I could have shouted over the roaring turbofans to reach my sulking sons, but didn't want to disturb the other passengers who must have ingested horse tranquilizers to actually sleep.

John Mark yammered. "You know," he said over the Irish Sea, "if there were no humans in the world the temperature would drop by two degrees?" My son, the prodigy. He smiled contentedly, inserted his earphones for the last quarter of the inflight movie, and deftly retook the armrest.

In 2010, I received a grant to cover a sabbatical from my duties as a Presbyterian pastor. Church members and grant readers liked my sabbatical plan: to follow my father's WWII footsteps from where he was captured in the Battle of the Bulge, to Glasgow, where he entered the war. My wife and sons would hopscotch with me from Liège, to Paris, Normandy, London, and Scotland, logging about a thousand miles in trains, taxis, elevators, boat, and on foot.

In the months before we left, ruminating about the trip got us antsy. The limits of time and money were no small part of my creeping unease. Having never been to Europe was another, adding not only mystique but also anxiety. Traipsing across the continent—a cliché to many of my well-traveled friends—wasn't old hat for me. This wasn't just another trip.

While we are a close family—actually eating dinner together nearly every night around the same table, with no phone or television or laptops edging in—the closer Europe got the more dinnertime squabbles bubbled up about trip details. Benjamin said he really wanted to go to Rome. Pops didn't go to Rome in the war, I explained. He was momentarily sullen, as if to say, *Why not? Since he was in the neighborhood, couldn't he have stopped by?* "What do you want to see in Rome, anyway?" I asked. *Paintings,* he insisted. I assured him the Louvre would offer more masterpieces than we could possibly absorb. He wasn't convinced. John Mark asked why we weren't going to Hawaii. Rachel was nervous about leaving her counseling clients in a lurch beyond the realm of a therapist's couch. Joseph, graduating high school just days before our journey's start, didn't want to miss the church's high school mission trip; it would be his last with his youth group. Benjamin didn't want to miss it, either; it would be his first with his older brother, whom he admired. John Mark asked if Europe had televisions; he didn't want to miss NCIS reruns. When Rachel told John Mark we were going to spend time together entertaining ourselves, he rolled his eyes.

We worried about my increasingly frail mother who lives with us in our home in South Carolina. We arranged for my sister to come stay with her. All would be well with Mom. But what about members of my congregation? What about the dog? The cat? The plants? Who would cut the grass?

Because so much was being invested, much could be lost. Risk loomed. A smidgen of trip-planning neurosis set in. I saw obstacles everywhere, everything from crashing planes to the difficulties of translating foreign restaurant menus. To keep costs down, we agreed we'd eat in at night. Mary Margaret, our trusted travel agent, told us that our apartments came equipped with small kitchens. And, she reminded us, we could practically survive on bread and cheese. Rachel and the boys agreed. Consuming nothing but bread and cheese, I envisioned constipation.

And what about getting something like a common case of pink eye? I could imagine the charades required to communicate to a French pharmacist the dire necessity for medicated eye drops. I only knew six French words and *buffet* doesn't have a declension for eye diseases. What about being kidnapped, wrapped in duct tape, and ending up at the center of an international incident? I practiced short speeches imploring our release, hoping their brevity would make for compelling sound bytes on CNN. If they flashed pictures on the screen of my lovely wife and handsome children, we might stand a chance.

When I let slip my heartburn over costs, John Mark brooded that the bank would repossess our house while we were gone. I told him that wouldn't happen and that he shouldn't fret, though, I realized, fretting might be in his genes. Besides, ours were just a few of the nearly $557 billion spent on leisure travel that would help strengthen the world economy. It helped a little to frame our journey in terms of philanthropy, but I still fretted.

Three weeks in close quarters spell a lot of togetherness. This pesky question, then, didn't surprise me, but it particularly nagged me: did I really want to spend three weeks cooped up on an unfamiliar continent with my three adolescent sons? I loved them, of course, but the indecision that often grips us about what channels to watch on TV might spell disaster when it came to deciding between bangers or mash, Left Bank or Right, or whether we needed the red line or green to get to the theater. I was aware, too, that my boys would not treasure every second hanging out with me—their boring, stupid dad. I could endure it, but could they?

This trip would require sacrifice from all of us. If we dared it, we'd be stuck with each other. There was a lot to feel nervous about.

And this was my greatest fear: that I'd be so moved in the Belgian woods in which my dad was captured that I'd begin to sob and not be able to stop. Ever.

My father's maternal side of the family, in the person of 17-year-old John Parramore, crossed the Atlantic Ocean in 1622. He and 153 other souls landed in Jamestown on the *Bonaventure*, a Virginia Company of London ship. According to the census of 1624/25, my six times great grandfather was a servant of a John Blore and sunk new world roots on Blore's 140-acre parcel located on Old Plantation Creek across the Chesapeake Bay on Virginia's Eastern Shore. Soon thereafter, Parramore had made it on his own as a planter near Magothy Bay. He incurred debt. Court records in 1634 ordered him to pay John Graves a hundred pounds of tobacco—the modern equivalent to a year-long membership at a health club. On at least one occasion he incurred the ire of the court, which, on June 9, 1638, ordered him to *sett by the heeles in the Stockes all the tyme of devyne service upon the next Sabboth day, For being drunk in the face of the Court.*

My father's earliest ancestor in the colonies may have been a bit of a rowdy, but he was good to his children. In a deed of gift dated June 3, 1650, Parramore, by now a widower whose first wife Jane *it hath pleased God to take to his mercie,* gave to their children Thomas, John, and Elizabeth the use of four cows. To Thomas and John he gave *one Indyan Boye called by the name of John.* Elizabeth got a feather bed with a rug and a set of sheets.

My dad's dad, Joe Matthews, came from Burlington, Vermont, having escaped the wrath of the Catholic nuns fond of rapping his knuckles. He joined the cavalry, graduated officer's candidate school in Plattsburg, NY, and made his way to Langley Field in what is now called Hampton, Virginia, where he courted a local girl. On October 2, 1918, he married her. Alice Hickman Parramore and he exchanged vows in a five o'clock ceremony at Hampton Baptist Church. Golden rod and evergreen adorned the sanctuary. Joe wore his uniform. The *Daily Press* reported that Alice's veil was "caught with orange blossoms." Officers from Langley lifted their swords for the newly married couple to walk under on their way to a honeymoon in Washington, DC, and Vermont. But they returned south after their wedding jaunt and never left. Hers was a Virginia family, and those roots held not only her husband, but their son, my dad, in Hampton virtually all their lives.

Five and a half years later, the Matthewses welcomed their third child into the world. William Parramore Matthews, my dad, was born in March, 1924, in Dixie Hospital five blocks away from their home at 68 Cherokee Road. Siblings Jimmy and Mary Louise were four and three when Billy made his entrance. Angeline would come next in 1927. A young Jimmy survived scarlet fever when Dad was a child, and when Paul and Jane Parramore got tuberculosis and went to the sanatorium in the mountains, Joe and Alice took in their little nephew Paulie. He was a year older than Dad and a well-suited playmate. He stayed a year. Joe and Alice's caboose and baby number five, little Alice, arrived in 1935.

Several dozen pictures from those earliest years survive. Two—of my father as a baby—stand out. My grandmother is holding Billy in her arms gazing at his serene, sleeping face. She is veritably lost in the looking. It is bliss. Every parent knows the feeling. In another, Dad's Granny sits in the yard in front of a trimmed hedge. She lived in a tiny cottage across the street and three houses down towards Chesapeake Avenue. She's holding Dad. Her hair is wound tight in a gray bun. She's looking at him with those same glassy-eyes as her daughter. He's awake in this picture, sitting like a prince in a white gown, with a bearing that says, "Yes, of course, I am the center of the known cosmos." As far as I ever saw, Dad was never haughty except in that photograph.

Mom says one reason she married Dad was for his big-hearted, exuberant family. My down to earth grandmother Alice let the kids dig in the backyard dirt with her sterling silver spoons. *Stuff* didn't matter to her. They welcomed all comers into their home. If another plate needed to be set for dinner, no problem. They laughed a lot. Joe required two things in terms of table etiquette. All would bow while he led a dinner prayer, and everyone had to stir sugar into their iced tea at the same time. After cessation of what for him was the nerve wracking clanging of spoons on glasses, conversation sweetened the evening. Folk then retired to the living room for *The Ziegfeld Follies of the Air*, or they strolled on sidewalks to the nearby Hampton Roads harbor.

Brownie snapshots show a family at ease. But Jim, strikingly broad and movie star handsome, looks serious in nearly every photo. What first-born weight did he bear on his linebacker shoulders? The girls all flash genuine smiles. Angeline looks a little shy. Baby Alice sits pretty in the crook of one or another sibling's arm in those early pictures. Joe Matthews is difficult to read. It's difficult to take a grown man seriously as he stands in the awkward, one-piece swimming garb of his day. He is thin with short hair that went snow white in his twenties. In one picture, he's in a winter coat and fedora with kids lined up before him at a tennis net; in another, he's holding one-year-old Dad protectively on top of a giant ball of snow. His expression reads like a slack tide. Not unlike a lot of fathers with one foot in the workaday world and another at home, his face reveals something either stern or amused. It's impossible to tell.

His wife's face is another story. Alice, eight years his junior, smiles like a quarter moon. She's beaming one of those generous smiles in the picture of her in a loose skirt wielding a baseball bat as if to say that her kids weren't going to have all of the fun. Like his mother, Billy Boy almost always smiled. And his eyes danced like hers.

The five kids had lots of friends in the neighborhood. Mary Virginia Peake and her two brothers lived next door; the Peakes were pillars in the Methodist church downtown. Irving Berlin (not the singer), who grew up to doctor much of the neighborhood, lived on the other side of the Matthewses in a house that his parents custom built from blueprints purchased from the Sears catalogue. Cousins Paulie and the McMenamins lived on the block. These and other children studied together and played every manner of game in the wide, shaded streets and in backyards. The girls played house, but also ball, like the boys. And everyone played on the water.

Half a block away, the Hampton Roads connected the Chesapeake Bay with the meandering James River, the largest of several rivers that find their terminus in the harbor. Harbor pilots like Mary Virginia Peake's dad guided the ships around the tricky Hampton Bar upriver to Newport News Shipbuilding or to the terminals on the Elizabeth River in Norfolk. The famed Captain John Smith and the lowly John Parramore first sailed that harbor three hundred years before. It was off this beach at the end of Cherokee Road where Dad learned to swim, crab, and dig clams with his toes.

In 1934, the family rented out their home in Hampton and moved eighty miles as the crow flies up the James River to Petersburg. Joe Matthews, still an Army captain, took command of the white Civil Conservation Corps Camp at Petersburg (camp 1364) followed by what was called the black camp at nearby Waverly (camp P-55, company 376). They lived at 1800 Chuckatuck Avenue, and high schooler Jimmy, handsome with a square jaw, dated nextdoor neighbor Helen Doyle. Still in grade school, Dad befriended Bobby Barton who lived down the street. They learned how to set campfires and tie every manner of knot in Cap Sailor's Boy Scout Troop. Dad played lots of tennis. A small kid for his age, the young Billy managed to smooth the clay courts near Wilcox Lake with a weighted roller in exchange for a few free sets. Maintaining tennis courts was the beginning of a lifetime of neighborly bartering in which Dad excelled. *I'll set the forms for your driveway if your concrete man will share his leftovers for my sidewalk.* Dad, never to be a manager of men, had only persuasion and grinning charm to get people to do things for him. It was a legitimate you-scratch-my-back, I'll-scratch-yours that got floor tiles laid, roofs shingled, and backyard gardens tilled. He was a pro at this sort of social and highly practical give and take.

His father had the weight of military rank to make things happen. While Dad rolled tennis courts at the park and sailed on the James River, Captain Matthews oversaw the construction of the camps and training of young men seeking respite from the Depression. He expected his men to be neat, to work hard, and to send money back home. They built stone walls and walks at the camps in order to create a home-like atmosphere. The men played music and relaxed with card games at night. By day, they landscaped the grounds—planting some of the 3 billion trees the CCC's are acclaimed to have planted across the nation. Captain Matthews and his 137 or so men did much to prepare the grounds at the nearby Petersburg National Battlefield as lands were added to the original Fort Stedman and Crater Battlefield properties.

Over 50,000 spectators gathered at the battlefield in April 1937 to reenact the infamous Battle of the Crater. Cadets from the Virginia Military Institute in Lexington, Marines, and National Guardsmen pretended to shoot each other and die while Douglass Southall Freeman, historian and *Richmond News Leader* editor, provided blow-by-blow narration. The crater, which still exists at the park, was 170- by 120-feet in circumference and 30-feet deep. In the summer of 1864, Union forces tunneled under the Confederate line defending Petersburg and ignited 320 kegs of gunpowder. The predawn blast maimed, killed, and stunned the Rebels, but Union troops didn't attack swiftly or expertly enough to make it around the crater, much less to the Jerusalem Plank Road which led to Petersburg. The battle was a blood bath. Five thousand men died. At the reenactment in 1937 they applauded and felt patriotic and ate fried chicken lunches on the grounds.

During his tenure, my grandfather was presented with a Union sword found in that crater. Brand new when the battle raged, the saber was made by Ames Manufacturing in Chicopee, Massachusetts, in 1864 and was unceremoniously handed down to my dad, minus the braided brass grip wrap that was probably unwound by Dad and all the cousins who played with it. It ended up stashed in the back of the attic when I was growing up. I wasn't allowed to play with it—for reasons I'm sure I could not comprehend—but I got to show it off to my awed friends. I could barely heft the thing, and it took a determined kid pulling from each end to yank it out of its tight-fitting scabbard. We swore we could make out flecks of dried blood on the curved silver blade. The blade was dull. The point was lethal. I imagined slashing and gouging the foe in battle. I would have been a killing machine.

The family moved back down the river to Hampton in 1938. Dad enrolled at George Wythe Junior High where he played on the Wythe Owl basketball team and tried to obey Miss Whaley in eighth grade homeroom. He learned his first notes on the sax in Adah Straus' Festival Band. It was a natural that Dad's smiling face belonged in the Glee Club. His ninth grade class prophecy foretold Billy Matthews becoming the "handsome idol of stage and screen." In the class last will and testament, Peggy Brittingham "left still telling jokes." Billy "left with the girls." Peggy signed his yearbook with either a challenge or a dare: "Behave yourself this summer, *if you can.*"

Perhaps Dad had some of John Parramore's rowdy blood in him. He was playful and charming, and one can imagine all of the things he could have gotten away with by flashing that ready, disarming smile. Compassion was part of his DNA, too. When a car hit schoolmate Bill Cameron at Hampton Roads Avenue and Kecoughtan Road, Dad spent hours playing chess with his convalescing friend. Neither boy would forget that bond. Dad also slept over most nights down the street at Granny's cottage. Who took care of whom is not certain, but Mr. and Mrs. Matthews didn't want Granny to be alone. Dad helped with evening chores. In the mornings he'd help make breakfast, then come home for his books before walking to school.

After his years as a Wythe Owl, Dad became a tenth grade cadet at Fork Union Military Academy, thirty miles south of Charlottsville. Cousin Paulie Parramore was already there; that probably was one reason Alice and Joe were willing to send their second son away. Bad grades were most likely another reason. Brother Jim, himself no star scholar, was at V.M.I. playing football despite being courted by Rip Miller, the assistant football coach at Navy. Jim got an appointment to Navy, but the scholarship wasn't much, so he took V.M.I. up on their full ride. Joe intended to pay the girls' college tuition, but Jim and my dad were expected to pay their way because they could—through R.O.T.C. or some other means open to men but not women. Joe would see to it that his girls would have the benefit of a college education. Mary Louise graduated with a teaching degree from Madison College in Harrisonburg, and when it was their turn, Angeline and little Alice would get their opportunity.

The Fork Union ads in *Boys Life Magazine* touted the campus' fireproof buildings and an indoor swimming pool. The boys ate well. A sample menu printed in the 1941-42 catalogue included fried oysters, sweet pickles, and corn bread. The rural town of Fork Union, the catalogue reported, was "made up of people of old Virginia stock, and it is exceptionally free from evils which are harmful to young people." One wonders if fellow senior Terry Kane—nicknamed "Killer"—had the administration's philosophy or the trustees' Baptist theology in mind when he signed Dad's yearbook with a stick figure standing below a halo. Killer said Dad was a great guy and a swell friend.

He may have been a swell fellow and "one of the best boys the South ever put out," as David "Doc" Fowley wrote, but Dad's high school grades did not improve; he was a lousy student. An English teacher, Jennings Springer, signed Dad's senior yearbook, the 1942 *Skirmisher*, suggesting he "keep up the tennis." English is one subject he passed, pulling an F in tenth grade up to a C in his final, eleventh grade. Ken Brock, a buff member of the wrestling team, wished Dad the best of luck passing trig. He didn't pass trig, but he eked by in history and algebra. He scored his best marks in Bible history and military tactics, ironic for a man who would later become fodder in one of the greatest tactical embarrassments in the history of the United States Army.

Dad was known for using his head in football, however, and he played a smooth saxophone in the band. He held the number two spot on the tennis team, closing out his senior season 3-2. At number one doubles, he and his partner were 4-2. In his senior picture in the yearbook, even though they misspelled his middle name, he looks confident and relaxed as if the future were paved with gold. Despite the string of deplorable grades that cratered his report cards, he graduated with his class on June first at the Wicker Chapel. Dr. Theodore F. Adams, pastor at First Baptist Church in Richmond, spoke to 93 graduates, and prayed over them. They needed it. Pearl Harbor had become a household name. The army was hiring. The war was on.

Dad returned to Hampton, and after a brief stint at the shipyard apprentice school in Newport News, he and fellow Wythe Owl alum J. P. Dale hopped the streetcar downtown and enlisted in the Army.

Walking on solid ground after deplaning at the Brussels National Airport was exhilarating. I relished using my legs again; there was a glad, rubbery bounce to my step, a feeling that I could easily dunk a basketball. In fact, I can barely launch myself high enough to touch the net. Morning air in the spacious halls hinted of the fresh outdoors and of freedom. Arrival's adrenaline fortified me with the needed courage to face Customs with some confidence. I secretly feared being detained for three days of tricky questioning. I practiced not saying words like *nitroglycerin*. Unlike my dad, I was not traveling with an army, just my family. And I didn't have a chain of command to look up to for assistance. Instead, my brood looked up to me. Acting like I knew what I was doing, I trembled at the prospect of letting them down.

I was embarrassed that I didn't know a word, not even an article or conjunction, of French, Dutch, Flemish, or German—all languages the armed agent was likely to speak. I pasted on a big smile and tried to look equal parts humble and thankful, hoping the agent would at least understand the gesture and cut me some slack. I wanted to hug him after he stamped my passport and, *in English*, said with a smile that I could go. All of us made it through, eliminating the need to debate how many of the family we could leave detained behind and still enjoy a worthwhile trip.

We huddled in the wide hallway behind customs and ticked off a list of what was next. An experienced tour guide would have been helpful at this moment. But everyone's eyes were on me. We needed to secure Euros, activate our train passes, visit restrooms, and discover how to get from Brussels to Liège. People did this all of the time. But not me. Never me. I felt like I was the first to have landed on the moon.

Liège—*the Athens of the north*—is as close as regular rail service can get us to the villages and forested countryside where the Battle of the Bulge was fought. Our guide Martin King would transport us from Liège to the battlefield. Martin and I had shared many emails over the twelve months prior to the trip. He knew the battlefront, the towns, the armies, the roads, the woods, and the reasons; we expected him and his seven-passenger minivan at our hotel after breakfast the day after we arrived.

But first we had to get out of the Brussels airport. The introduction with the cash machine proved a more difficult translation exercise than communicating with customs. The nice customs agent knew enough English to meet me half way. The cash machine did not. I waited behind an African and his testy female companion who was dressed like a model and seemed either disinterested, angry, or both. In a language I did not understand, he asked her what appeared to be reasonable and polite questions over his shoulder while he punched in numbers on the machine. In a language that did not sound like his, she answered curtly. He wore designer shoes. She slumped against a washing machine-sized suitcase on Barbie wheels. Was this relational discord a foreshadowing of what soon might befall us? Hoping she understood my marital shorthand, I looked at Rachel and stretched my face into a wide, forced smile.

Rachel and I managed to push a combination of right buttons, and successfully follow French-language prompts. Our credit card worked. The machine spat out neat stacks of Euros that resembled pretend currency from a Parker Brothers board game. Mission accomplished. Next stop was the train.

The man downstairs at the train counter seemed genuinely glad to see me. I appointed my 18-year-old Joseph to stand with me at the window and asked him to make sure I was doing everything okay. Reluctantly, he agreed. He didn't, actually, have a choice. I needed him. The rest of the family huddled along the wall near the most wanted posters. Though we packed light, our suitcases had multiplied. Benjamin, John Mark, and Rachel stood amidst the pile of strewn cases like roadies for The Rolling Stones.

Fathers shamelessly filch from their children. When he was younger, I'd swiped a few twenties from Joseph's piggy bank on numerous date nights without thinking. Any of my children almost always have more cash than me. I've always paid them back. But this was different. Now, I dared to borrow something from my eldest that I could hardly name and possibly never repay. I needed him to standby, even with an aloof, teenaged nonchalance. What I needed more was his belief that I could do this on my own. His confidence might lend the oomph my sagging spirit needed.

I wondered if Dad ever leaned on me without me knowing it. According to his high school transcript, Joseph is alleged to have satisfactorily passed three years of German. If the man at the ticket booth spoke French but not English, I would look to Joseph to attempt German. Naturally, one would expect a French functionary to speak German. Joseph didn't know that I was thinking this, of course. He made clear to us long before leaving the States that we had better not look to him for translation services because he wasn't going to render any.

And he was serious. But his high school German completed only three weeks prior—if needed—would prove a lot more useful than my rusty memory of high school Spanish taken thirty years ago. If I needed it, I would ask him to help. I was serious, too. Desperately so.

Besides possibly needing his language skills with the ticket agent, I needed another set of ears and eyes to help me keep things straight. He's good at detail. I also needed another human being nearby for moral support. I was glad for Joseph. He's growing into his six-foot frame, lacking the hard angles of adulthood, but getting close.

The ticket agent handled my wad of tickets and receipts like a Vegas black jack dealer, stamping what needed to be stamped, and signing and dating the necessary blanks. My dad always appreciated watching somebody do something well; he passed this down to me. The agent's hands flashed through the flipping pages. His English was excellent. He was authentically personable. We made small talk. I said "merci" *a lot.*

"You're very welcome," he said magisterially. "It is no problem."

I wanted him to know that I was not just another Ugly American demanding that the whole universe speak my language. While I had day dreamed my way through my final semester of Spanish nearly thirty years earlier, my *intention* to master a linguistic United Nations was heart-felt. I wanted this competent man to know how grateful I was for his service, grateful that the long flight had ended, grateful to the nation of Belgium for letting me enter, and grateful in advance for the train that would whisk my family away to Liège.

"Track number three," he said, pointing around his enclosure to the glass doors to my left. "To Leuven." If it weren't for the sheet of riot-proof glass separating us I would have kissed him on both cheeks. Belgians like that. Or is that the French?

Seeing that no kissing was possible, I just waved, bowed, and uttered "merci" three times, identical triplets of heart-felt relief and sincere appreciation. I hoped Joseph noticed what an international wheeler-dealer I was. I had navigated

Customs, correctly pushed the French-language buttons on a cash machine, and gotten a green light to board one of the best train systems in the world. I waved confidently for my family to follow me. They hardly had enough arms for the luggage. We were on our way.

We settled onto the train that rocketed beyond the asphalt roads and grey buildings of Brussels into the rolling green hills and yellow fields of the countryside. Weariness overcame me almost to the point of circulatory shock; we rocked sleepily into each other's soft bodies as we wended through colored fields. Trees with new leaves swished by in a hypnotic blur. The rails skirted vowel-rich towns such as Tienen, Exemaal, and Neerwinden, where we made brief stops. By noon, we eased into the Liège-Guillemins rail station where the escalators ran like silver streams of water and the arching concrete roof soared like seagulls in flight.

We secured a taxi near the station. The twenty-something driver, in training for Le Mans, whipped around curves and shot through packs of slower, coughing cars. Velocity and dull fear pressed us into the grimy upholstery. The spire of St. Paul's Cathedral reaching up into blue sky reminded me that God is God of the whole cosmos, and by extension, the roadways. In less than ten minutes we jolted to a stop at the curbside of Hotel Mercure. Having already arranged our bags in a perfect line on the sidewalk, our driver helped us stagger out of the taxi. In a moment, he was gone and we stood looking up at our hotel. This was it. For four nights, this flag bedecked low rise was home away from home.

Early in my trip planning, I had decided not to trace Dad's steps as a POW into Germany for two reasons. First, I didn't think we would have enough time to do justice to such a trip. Second, Dad remembered so few geographic specifics that I feared we'd get tangled in a wild goose chase. German prison camps late in the war were all full, so prisoners captured at the Bulge very often had no place to go. POWs occupied boxcars and were carted across Germany on trains. Where there were no rails, they marched.

They slept where they could. Josephine Bovill, a nurse in the 77th Field Hospital at Camp Lucky Strike at Saint Sylvian near Le Havre on the French coast, said of all the prisoners she dealt with after the war (and some 73,000 streamed through Lucky Strike),[1] Bulge prisoners were the most physically pathetic. They had been marching nearly non-stop for four months with very little food. They were gaunt, skin-and-bone ghosts of their former selves.[2]

John Kline, a machine gunner from Terre Haute serving in the 423rd "M" Company, writes of being constantly marched around Germany. His journal records the conditions on the train from Stalag XII-A in Limburg to IV-B in Muhlberg in Brandenberg (where Dad remembers spending one night). The trip took Kline six nights and seven days. "We did not get out of the box-cars during the whole trip. Our toilet facility for 60 men was a 5 gallon bucket. We were fed only three times during the trip. A slice of bread and a small, very small portion of cheese, water only twice. We used a can on a string to scoop snow from the tracks."[3]

Dad remembered sleeping in churches, graveyards, and barns, but he had no clue in what cities or towns these makeshift accommodations were. The brick factory that he remembers may have been in Duderstadt, what Kline called a "hell hole" crammed with 4,000 prisoners. "It was four stories in height with one narrow staircase. Each floor was piled high with clay bricks that had not yet been 'baked' in the kiln. Dust settled through the spaces on the wooden floors, as well as urine and excrement from the diarrhea infested men who could not wait to go outside."[4]

Paul Peterson, also from Dad's 106th, included in Thomas Saylor's oral history this remembrance about Duderstadt. He and a walking buddy, Bert Doane from Sioux Falls, South Dakota, shared a single "awful German ersatz blanket" made with wood chips. "Neither of us were in very good condition by that time, toward the end of the march. One morning I woke up, and Bert didn't."[5]

Besides the brick factory, Dad hazily remembered Stalag VIII-A, but he couldn't be sure. He also remembered Stalag IV-B in Muhlberg, for which I have documentation of his presence; I don't know when he was there. As unbelievable as it sounds, Dad remembered being in only those two stalags, and only there one night each. The rest of the time they were crammed in boxcars, marching, or in the ruins of bombed buildings.

My family would explore Germany another time.

Instead, we would trace Dad's steps from the Belgian-German border to Paris. Dad was hospitalized there—or near there—after repatriation. Mom remembers him talking about the tower of Notre Dame. If our plans unfolded as meticulously as they were conceived, we'd stand in that tower and look upon the city as he may have done.

We'd make our way to the English Channel on an air-conditioned tour bus through hedgerows to Normandy. Dad crossed the channel from England on a ferry to the docks at Le Havre. The beaches and national cemeteries would remind us of the men who cleared the way, who took the coast, and opened east-west roads like the Red Ball Highway. After five nights in Paris, we'd take the Euro Star to London.

A quick jaunt to Edinburgh and Glasgow would be next. The plan called for finding a ferry that would get us on the Firth of the River Clyde where the RMS Aquitania dropped Dad off. In his unpublished war journal, Sgt. Kenneth Grant of an anti-tank platoon in the 422nd wrote about the "cute houses along the shore." It was a far cry from his hometown of Detroit where he was a lathe operator at the DeSoto Automobile Plant on Jefferson Avenue. "In the background there are high mountains and the tops of them are covered with snow."

Traveling in June, we'd miss Europe's winter. We'd miss the snow that made important roads on the battlefront simply disappear, much to the desperation of men lost in the woods fleeing for their lives, searching for others in their shot-up, separated units. We'd miss the fear that gripped both the Flemish farmers who lived in range of screaming memmies and Waffen SS raids, and London merchants who faced V2 rockets and Stuka bombers. We'd miss the fear, the hunger, the cold, the bleeding dysentery, the exhaustion.

Thank God we'd miss all that.

But we wouldn't miss the London Eye, Westminster Abbey, or a host of other tourist attractions. Thanks to Mom's generosity, we had tickets for Andrew Lloyd Webber's *Love Never Dies* at the Adelphi; huge Webber fans, the boys couldn't wait. Sure, we'd traipse through some battlefields and graveyards, but we'd also eat croissants hot from the ovens of Parisian cafes, British fish and chips, Belgian chocolate.

And I would be able to enjoy what Dad couldn't. I wouldn't have to contend with wooden Schu landmines and snipers. I would be able to walk where Dad had walked, except at a leisurely pace. A bed with clean sheets would await me in a nearby hotel. I could hold my wife's hand and watch my kids zing a Frisbee back and forth, scoping out members of the opposite sex. No forty pound barracks bag, no C rations and canteen, no rifle, no ammunition clips, no snow, no worries.

After speed-naps at the Hotel Mecurer and sandwiches at the lobby snack bar, we attempted a stroll to test our legs still vibrating from flight. Those flags of unfaded, primary colors danced lazily from second stories of the white, blue, and yellow buildings that curved gracefully along the Boulevard de la Sauveniere. We wandered through narrow, cobbled shopping alleys to the winding Meuse River. One of Hitler's objectives in the Battle of the Bulge was to capture the bridges over the Meuse on his way to Antwerp. I just wanted to stand by it. When we stopped in the middle of the pedestrian bridge and looked back, the city practically struck a pose for us beneath dramatic slants of evening sun.

The best sight of all, though, was my family. The light may have been playing tricks on me because my sons looked a bit like my father—those Matthews' lips and bold noses— and they looked distinctly like themselves, too, boys just a few moments away from manhood. A relaxed Benjamin leaned on the bridge rail gazing up river. Rachel was taking a picture of me while I was taking a picture of her. Our kids were clustered around her. John Mark was her size. Joseph and Benjamin, between growth spurts at around six feet, dwarfed her by eight inches. When did this happen?

Did I see relief in their eyes? Were they thinking as I was: *We've made it all the way across the ocean. We're finally here.* Walking had begun to help me feel connected to the earth again, released from the claustrophobic suspension of transatlantic flight, the spinning of time zones, the drone of jet engines. Fresh air, sun, and seeing my family's faces were bringing me gently back to earth. The honey colors of a lingering evening sun flowed through the streets. Rooftops reflected the light in such a way that there were no clean lines. Cityscape and sky blurred together, a melding of things made by human hands and of elements that were not. Behind these four shining faces, I couldn't tell where sky ended and earth began.

3

Blood and Guts

For seven years, beginning when I was in third grade, we lived at number two Maynard Street in a house that sat less than ten-feet from the Hampton Roads Harbor. After nor'easters, Dad would haul out the garden hose to spray off seaweed from the upstairs windows before the sun baked it on. Ours was the only house I knew that got washed. In those summer evenings, Dad spent hours unwinding in Indian River Creek that ran next to our house. As a kid, I never understood what adults had to unwind about. They had it easy. They could stay up late. They could drive cars. They could eat ice cream out of the box.

Dad glided ankle-deep in the water and paid exquisite attention to what lurked in those muddy-green shallows. His crab net was an extension of himself. He dipped it into the water without making ripples. His feet, clad in cheap, old tennis shoes, never broke the surface. This he learned from herons.

On the evening I'm thinking of, he jerked the net up, twisting the handle in a single, skilled movement as if it had become a poisonous snake. Tangled inside the net was a big, fighting jimmy—a male crab. He was hoping for a soft crab, no doubt, which he would clean on the dock and take inside for Mom to fry in half a stick of butter sputtering in the cast iron skillet that I hardly had the strength to lift. Unless he was in a serious mood for crabbing and a very late dinner, he'd let this lucky hard crab go. Catching a mess of crabs was the easy part, but steaming and picking them was tedious no matter how much you savored the meat.

This jimmy was a beaut, which is why Dad sloshed across the creek to show him off. He waded out of the narrow channel onto the apron of sand on our side of the creek. Smiling his boyish grin, he looked up at me. He was pleased as punch.

"Looky here," he bragged, holding up the net.

He reached in to the tangled mesh to pinch the blue crab at the base of its swimming legs and pick him up, just like he had taught me to do but that I was—at that age—always too chicken to try. Even though Dad was an old pro, the determined crab managed to pinch *him*, hard, in the fleshy meat between the thumb and forefinger. His tan hand went red with blood; the blue claw with its saw-line of white teeth had latched on like a vise.

Another man would have cussed, but Dad just winced, flailed his hand once, twice, flicking the tenacious crab off. The body went flying into the creek while the claw remained clamped onto Dad's bleeding hand.

I wanted to help him. Sitting on that hot concrete seawall with my legs dangling, I wanted to do something. I was almost nine. I wanted to ease his pain. He looked up at me with wet eyes and that same I'm-not-kidding, undiminished smile. He had jammed the handle of the net under his arm and with his good hand was prying loose the claw from the other.

Just a minor inconvenience, he seemed to be saying as he gingerly finagled the claw off, pumped his fist, then wiggled his sticky, red fingers. He could have been grazed by an eighteen-wheeler. *All in a day's work,* he seemed to be saying. *Everything's okay. Everything's going to be all right.*

It was with this sort of practical nonchalance that this man of few words spoke of the war. *The war is over,* he seemed to say, *and this perfect low tide won't wait.*

Was there space inside my dad's head, a holy of holies to which I could be allowed to enter, shoes off, head bowed? I wondered with Whitman, "Of hard-fought engagement or sieges tremendous what deepest remains?"

"Win some, lose some," he said. His shoes oozed water as he squished his way across soft sand to the ladder at the dock.

He doled out answers about the war like some men play poker. He never let his expression betray his hand. The United States Office of War Information papered stateside bus stops and public places with *Loose Lips Sink Ships* and other posters. Dad took those words to heart long after VE Day.

"What was war like?" I'd ask.

"It was very, very cold."

The harder I pushed, of course, the less I got. Most of what I discovered of Dad's war experiences I acquired quite by accident. If Dad felt a nap coming on when reading the Sunday Daily Press-Times Herald in his recliner, and if it were chilly, he'd slyly place sections of the paper over him from his ankles up to his belly.

"Why don't you just get an afghan?" I'd ask. My maternal grandmother and other women in my family went through a crocheting stage, and we had a dozen, perhaps ten thousand, outrageously colorful afghans draped across nearly every chair-back. Dad looked at me like mine was the dumbest question in the world.

"Because I'd have to get up," he'd say.

Well of course. No use ruining a good nap by actually getting out of your chair for an afghan. "But *newspapers* can't actually keep you warm," I said.

He looked at me not unkindly.

"Sure they can," he gently corrected. "In the war, what do you think we *did* with newspapers?"

I flushed with embarrassment. To this day I still haven't gotten my head around the odd fact that my dad sought warmth beneath the pages of the local news and grocer's ads. That's how the war came up, a puzzle piece finding a rare fit. Insight came like water on the moon, and always quite unexpectedly.

Back in the day when bread machines were all the rage, Uncle Jim—an artillery man stationed in Aachen on the northernmost shoulder of the Bulge when Dad was 50 miles south near St. Vith—went through a bread-making stage. Those were Jim's heftier days. Every time we saw him and Aunt Ginny, he proudly presented a sturdy loaf of his newest recipe. As far as I knew, the man hadn't heated up a can of soup his whole life before becoming a machine-assisted, gourmet baker. I could not tell the difference between one heavy loaf and another. I said as much to my parents once after Uncle Jim and Aunt Ginny had cruised away in their green Chrysler New Yorker for their home in nearby Williamsburg. Dad noted, offhandedly, "It sure beats the tree flour they fed us when I was a prisoner of war."

Huh?

I looked it up. *Tree Flour* was a German euphemism for saw dust. One recipe for the black bread he ate as a POW called for 50-percent bruised rye grain, 20-percent sliced sugar beets, 20-percent tree flour (saw dust), 10-percent minced leaves and straw.[6] That and a watery barley soup once every other day—if he were lucky—provided a feast in the winter of 1944-45. More than once he ate moldy German pie and scraps from the garbage and was glad to have it.

My childhood was pocked by rare bombshells like tree flour and newspaper blankets. Once, I was blind-sided by lice infestation and chemical showers. Another time it was beriberi and starvation. The man who could magically disappear at the hint of family conflict could also pull a loaded bazooka out of a hat. He didn't talk about his frostbitten toes, but his careful tending of them spoke volumes. These yellowed-brown, thick toenails looked like petrified bark. I remember thinking that he should take better care of them. In fact, they required exquisite care from a podiatrist, especially in later years when he couldn't bend over to do it himself. Now and then he groused about having to pay for the American Red Cross doughnuts and coffee in England; troops aren't charged money they don't have for basics like coffee and doughnuts. It infuriated him. He never donated to the Red Cross because of that, even though, when he starved in German captivity, Red Cross chocolate bars helped keep him alive.

He seldom spoke about any of it: Training at Ft. Sill. Missing home. Never knowing what was next. The feeling you have when you were freezing to death. The fear of dying, killing, blushing. The special agony of tears. Dad was one of millions of witnesses. Perhaps his silence said it all. But what, exactly, did the silence say? While the silences may have been profound—even holy—for my dad, for me they were both puzzling and terrifying. Dad may have been confounded by the heartbreaking and utter stupidity of words. I was confounded by the lack of them.

When I was a kid, I ached for Dad to tell me gory war stories, how in the heat of battle blood boiled and brave men did brave things. I imagined my dad in that cauldron of fire. The movies and their stars came to mind. *Tora, Tora, Tora! The Dirty Dozen. The Guns of Navarone.* I saw my own father in the smooth machismo of John Wayne, in the grimy face of Lee Marvin, and in the snarl of a young Clint Eastwood. But nothing could have been a wider visual or behavioral disconnect. Dad had big ears, kind eyes, and an easy laugh.

One beloved family friend, Helen Scallion, said he was simple. "You know what I mean, Matt," she said after he died. "I don't mean to say he was stupid, but he just wasn't complicated." She was right. He wasn't dark or brooding. He liked jokes. He was curious and outgoing. He said "dagnabbit" when he purpled his thumb with a 20-ounce claw hammer.

All I wanted was a front-line once-upon-a-time action story. Blood, guts, gore.

"You don't want to hear about *that mess*," he'd say.

But I did. I did want to know. How disappointed I was that Dad didn't oblige my direst wish. It shames me now to admit this, but when I was in grade school I wondered *What was wrong with him?* His unwillingness to talk forced me to resort to what kids often have to do: tap into my imagination. And I only had the movies to go by—the movies and Dad's steely silence.

I had a crush on my second grade teacher, Mrs. Parish. She quieted a hacky cough once by swigging Robitussin right from the bottle in front of the class. I loved her. In show and tell one day, I talked about my dad and the war. When I said, "My dad killed Germans in the war," everyone's eyes got round, including Mrs. Parish's. Since I had so little to go on, I had no choice but to make everything up.

Mrs. Parish certainly knew I didn't know what I was talking about. And just as certainly, I suspect, she hoped I never would know. She didn't comment on one of my earliest attempts to wield a war story, but she did later put her arm around me at my desk and show me that the word *math* and my first name were spelled almost exactly the same. This astonished me. My affinity for mathematics beyond that sweet moment, however, did not flourish.

Mom, Dad, and I were living thousands of miles and two decades distant from the war, which Dad tried so hard to forget. Sisters Susan and Carol had married and moved away before I was in third grade; more than a decade older than I, they observed the unspoken rule never to bring up *that mess*. We had a nice life. I had stacks of clean clothes nicely folded in a solid-wood dresser from Brittingham's Furniture, carpet on the floor, a kitchen full of food, a toy box filled with colored blocks. I had a stay-at-home mom content on building a life with my dad, which never included interrogating him about the war. On that front, she was his reliable *résistance Française.*

In seventh grade I wanted to connect my dad's story with what I had been discovering in history class at C. Alton Lindsey Junior High. I was learning about the rudiments of research and the importance of primary sources. Dad was a primary source. He was my very own artifact. None of my friends' dads had fought in WWII.

Ken, a Vietnam vet at Community Presbyterian Church in which I grew up, wasn't shy about telling people war stories. But even he would get right up to a point and put on the brakes. He'd talk about the geography, the armies, the politics. But when it came to the actual battle I remember his growing suddenly quiet and the whole room with him. His law partner Rick Hardwick, one of our youth group leaders, would deftly change the subject. Even though I didn't fully understand what was going on then, I knew that everybody needed a friend like Rick Hardwick.

As I grew into my teens, I began to pay more attention to the world's pain on the TV news. I'd watch my dad watching. He'd often wince away from what he saw. "I don't understand this mess," he'd say as we watched footage of killings and riots and grieving people. "Senseless." He was a man in a vice.

I hurt for him. Nothing he did or said invited this. I just felt it, and I felt it powerfully.

I ached that Dad had to go to war, that he had to see and do what he saw and did. Can posttraumatic stress disorder skip a generation? Did he know how I grieved for him? Did he know how I lamented his lost youth? Had I found both the courage and actual words to say those things, I think I know exactly what he would have told me. "You do what you have to do."

Win some, lose some.

When I was sitting on the seawall watching him poke around in the creek at low tide, I wanted a war story and got silence instead. When I was 19—Dad's age when he dug his first foxhole in a war zone—I wanted the same thing, but I wanted it for different reasons. I cared about him—not the war, not the guts, not the gore. That's why I wanted to know what he did in the army, how he felt about the war, where he was located on the front, who he met along the way, how battle rattled him, what his captors were like, and where they took him as a POW. I was curious about how he lived with the memory of war while insulated in the upholstered comfort of middle class America. I wanted, more than anything, to connect with my father.

This verbal inquiry yielded such unsatisfying results. It was too much pressure for both of us. Maybe we needed to rebuild a Chevy or clear some land together. The story might have come out better that way, in snippets of side conversations—telling the truth, but telling it *slant*. I lacked the sophistication to know that then. Regardless, Dad had lashed down the memories so well and tightly, that the knots had hardened. I wouldn't learn until it was too late that getting at the story required less muscle and more finesse.

As a pastor, I've had talks with other vets that were long and rich. I'd ask a few questions and it was like I'd turned on a faucet. They'd talk and talk. They'd tell funny stories, bawdy stories, go briefly silent when the killing and dying came up, wipe the water from their eyes, talk about how good it was to come home and how glad they were that it ended. Afterwards a wife or a grown daughter would catch me on the driveway as I was leaving. They'd say things like, "I'm pretty sure that you're the first person he has ever talked to about the war." Or, "I learned more in 90 minutes about Dad's war experience than I have since I've known him."

My own father? Maybe he wanted to protect us both— he in the telling and me from the hearing. No scary stories, bedtime or otherwise. No unpleasant thoughts. To pause for reflection might risk getting *stuck* like so many poor souls who couldn't forget the war or function afterwards. Before the first major antipsychotic drug Thorazine hit the market in the mid-1950s, VA doctors lobotomized 1,464 men after the war to curb their flashbacks.[7] The American Psychiatric Association (APA) published the first mental illness diagnostic manual in 1952, the *Diagnostic and Statistical Manual I (DSM-I)*, in which they coined the term "Gross Stress Reaction" to replace what the Army had called *Shell Shock* and *Battle Fatigue*.[8] The term *Post Traumatic Stress* had yet to be invented. Dad lumped all the euphemisms and slogans about war and its effects into a simpler phrase: *That Mess*.

No, safer to move on, and to keep moving. *Besser ein End emit Schrecken als ein Schrecken ohne Ende*, as his German captors might have said. *Better an end with horror than a horror without end.* No need to open old wounds; absolutely no reasonable person would relive a past like that. No need, even, to talk about it. That mess.

Maybe he didn't want to be my case study, hero, or my history teacher. Maybe this is one of these things sons have to figure out for themselves, so he stood by not so much engaged in my wonderings as present to them, ready to pass the second helping of mashed potatoes at the dinner table every single night, but otherwise aloof about this puzzle I was trying to piece together. Perhaps he just wanted to be my dad.

My desire to learn about his war experiences truly perplexed my old man. He really didn't understand why I wanted to know about what he wanted to forget. Equal parts befuddlement and frustration were ingredients of our relationship, particularly on this front. Is this true for every father? Every son?

In our kitchen one day, in my thirties, he read over a Memorial Day essay I had written about him for the local newspaper. He was impressed, grateful, and characteristically stymied. "Why do you want to know all this mess?"

"I just do," I replied weakly. I wasn't articulate enough then to say I didn't put these life-long questions in my brain in the first place. It wasn't my fault I was so curious to know. Dad couldn't know how the questions burned for the salve of his answers. I never knew how to tell him that.

And I couldn't say the most obvious thing of all.

I loved him.

4

Midnight Is A Place

John Mark was joking about the size of our coffee cups at breakfast in Liège. They held three shots of very black coffee. "Look how tiny they are," he said. "They aren't even normal." What did he know about cups, much less coffee?

This java was the hard stuff. Had it been an American supersized, it would stagger a horse. The boys cut it with shots of thick cream and packets of sugar. "Cheers," we'd all say, delicately clinking together the sturdy but small white ceramic cups. Freedom from the cramped quarters of Delta's third class and the caffeine electrified our party mood.

Nothing was cramped or rationed at this table. We slurped indelicately. The joke would be on us, of course, if we kept slugging this stuff down. If the morning caffeinated jitters didn't get us, the afternoon crash might. "Bottoms up," we jested, and lifted our third round. John Mark may have been on his fourth.

We were still dulled by our flight of fewer than 24 hours before, but the day was bright, and we were eager to get out in it. Breakfast in this sunny dining area off the smart lobby at the Mercure was a great beginning. Platters of scrambled country eggs, slices of salami and prosciutto, flakey croissants whose fluffy white centers were dotted with melting Belgian chocolate, slices of bacon and fruit covered buffet tables dressed in starched, white linen. Hotels lose money on free breakfasts with families like ours. Our boys ate like footballers. The brunette waitress left another generous pot of coffee on our small table, whisking away the empty. We smiled, and I said "merci" a little too loudly, relishing the sound of such an enchanting word twisting off my tongue. Solitary men in business suits sat together, leaning over plates of food while glancing at headlines in the *Het Laatste Nieuws* and the *Wall Street Journal*. I wondered if they missed their families back home. I was so glad to be with mine.

The boys beamed as they munched and laughed. Benjamin's ready smile revealed braces and a dimple that will drive girls wild. Right now it was just cute. Soon it will be dangerous. They downed the coffee like college freshmen with fake IDs might knock down pints. Rachel giggled at them, leaning back as she often does, as if to frame them in some wider perspective. Joseph delicately poured another round. Putting on airs, John Mark lifted his cup ceremonially. We lifted ours. "Cheers," he announced. We clinked cups and sipped. It was hot, even with cream.

Our day's tour guide whom I was eager to meet was due in half an hour. He was going to take us in his van to the front an hour away where the Battle of the Bulge began. Unlike the ballet of men in pinstripes, we were in no rush. My family returned for seconds and thirds from the buffet. It was John Mark's birthday. He was twelve. That deserved another toast. Five? Six?

We were giddy and full. Rachel had sipped her coffee and was enjoying a conservative second cup. The boys and I had consumed a few more cups, plus orange juice. We pushed back from the table having hoovered its contents. I wanted to bask a bit more, but the boys yawling like sea lions had grown impatient. Ben's foot bounced supersonically under the table; it was perhaps beyond his control. He asked politely, "Are we ready?" We were.

With a few minutes before our guide was to arrive, we crammed into the small elevator. We grabbed our stuff from our rooms, then crowded back inside the cozy elevator. Our boys smelled of mint and Old Spice. It was a glorious morning high. Everyone smelled good.

A fit, leprechaun of a man wearing an eager grin and an olive army jacket stood like a fire hydrant in the lobby. Young businessmen jostled around him leaving the breakfast buffet for taxis. Martin King. I recognized him from the internet. His short hair and goatee were prematurely white. A silver Celtic cross necklace hung high on his chest, atop a black muscle shirt. He wore black pants, and the collar was fashionably flipped up on his vintage jacket. A Union Jack was emblazoned over his right pocket. In a rumpled kind of way, he exuded what my boys might call *swag*.

"You must be Matthew," he said in a Highland brogue, eagerly offering his hand. His grip was surprisingly firm. Narrow glasses magnified curious, friendly eyes. I introduced him to my family as though we had enjoyed a boyhood friendship instead of computer correspondence. He shook each boy's hand hard, but took Rachel's hand gently and bowed. Men in suits slipped between us like penguins. The orderly lobby buzzed with human traffic. As if someone had pressed an "on" button, Martin launched into a animated talk about the Battle of the Bulge to everyone who cared to listen. Using the full extension of his arms to the tips of his fingerprints, and rocking up upon his toes to his full, elfish height he talked of *"heroes like Matthew's dear father."* I might be annoyed if someone else spoke of my father like that without ever having known him, but Martin pulled it off. He was telling the story of a man I had always wanted to know better.

My boys wore shocked, wooden expressions but edged cautiously, nevertheless, to the center of the crowd. They glanced back and forth from my face to Martin's. I sensed they were scanning my face for clues about how to take this jovial guy. They saw that I was spellbound. But did they also notice that I discretely rubbed the corner of each eye? I was not flicking away sleep, but what I anticipated might be the first of many tears.

Talk of Dad triggered in me a sudden sadness. Despite the caffeine and the excitement of standing at the trailhead of what promised to be an exciting day, I felt myself go a little limp. People tell me in their grieving that they pick up the phone and dial their loved one before they realize their father or mother or son has been dead for weeks, even for years. And it all comes back to them like it just happened, like an emotional curveball to the forehead. Their loved one is really gone. Martin was telling me about my own father and it stung that Dad was not here in the lobby with us, on this earth. Dad would have immediately liked Martin. Martin would have lavished attention on him and Dad would have lapped it up. Sure, Dad wouldn't have shared Martin's enthusiasm for talking about the war he tried to forget, but he wouldn't have minded basking for a moment in Martin's hero-worship liturgy.

An equally unexpected affection for my sons welled up in me as they began to relax in Martin's presence. This surprised me, also. I *am* a schmaltzy man, but it usually takes more than a full minute with a total stranger for me to get teary. *Oh, brother.* Maybe it was the jet lag.

Martin spoke expansively about the weather on the 1944 morning of December 16—the day the battle began—of mists, snow, sleet. He spoke of the landscape, Hitler's battle plan. Then, he darted back to the present, leaned into our little huddle, and asked the boys what they called their grandfather. Joseph spoke up, one word that I hadn't heard him say in a long time. *Pops.* Martin seemed to make mental note of their ages, especially that today was John Mark's birthday, to which he lifted his white eyebrows.

He straightened to his full height. "I am Scottish, born and bred—*long live the Queen*—and I married a Dutch woman who takes real good care of me," he said with a wink. We laughed. He chatted a moment about the history films he consults on. "I feel like a star on those film sets," he said. "They pamper me, they do. But when I get home, my wife knocks me down a peg or two." We laughed again. Martin must have aced Tour Guide School.

He fell silent, cocked his head, folded his hands into a semblance of prayer, and held us in his dramatic pause. He leaned in closer, and my boys and Rachel met him halfway, heads almost touching in our ever-tightening circle. The businessmen made wide berth en route to front desk, elevator, or taxis. I halfway expected something from the 1637 *Scottish Book of Common Prayer*. He whispered, "All conditions and armies had come together in a perfect storm. The Germans cut through the thinly defended allied line like a knife through soft butter. They wreaked their holy hell. And men like your brave Pops—*Matthew's dear father*—were right in their way."

We broke huddle. Hands by his side, open palms, and a *why not?* look, he nodded toward the glass lobby doors to his illegally parked minivan. "But let's get on with it, shall we?" My kids, considerably more relaxed now, followed him outside like he was a favorite uncle. Rachel looked relieved. I couldn't have been happier.

I rode shotgun. Martin zipped through busy local traffic and within minutes vistas opened. We were leaving Liège behind for the hilly, forested Ardennes. It is too rugged here for big farms. The highway wasn't crowded.

"I've driven this van all the way to Russia," Martin announced with another practiced wink. My astonishment must have registered, because he laughed when he glimpsed me in his peripheral vision. "But, you understand, that's only a thousand miles."

Europe seems like it *ought* to be bigger. A thousand miles wouldn't quite get me from my house in South Carolina to my in-laws' house. To think the Russian border is closer to Martin's house in Antwerp than Austin, Texas, is to mine boggled my mind. How can so many countries, languages, old hatreds, loyalties, and cultures fit into a region only slightly bigger than the United States? Charles de Gaulle wondered similarly about France. "How can one conceive of a one-party system in a country that has over two hundred varieties of cheese?"

We made good time on the *Autosnelwegen*-602 to Bastogne. In our emails back and forth in the prior 10 months, I had told Martin as much as I knew about Dad's position near St. Vith at the middle of the 90-mile battle front. He knew that I wanted my boys to leave with a general sense of the battle. I trusted him with the details. Bastogne was near the southern shoulder of the battle. Gentle valleys, fields, and the occasional castle blurred past. He conducts one tour a month, mostly with those who fought in the war and have come back to see the battlefield before they die. He explained how they stroll through the quiet woods, heads down like men who have lost a coin in the grass, talking in low, thin voices about what it was like half a century ago, in winter, in snow. These old guys get out to stretch their legs, look around, try to fit an old barn or odd bend in the road into the set of frozen images they carry in their heads like brittle antiques or gold-leaf icons. Martin said he watches the light go on in their eyes as they nod—or flinch—when recognition dawns. "I've done this dozens of times," Martin said. "It's an honor to accompany these fine, fine gents."

After 40 minutes, we left the highway for smaller roads. We got out in the woods above the village Foy and traipsed around foxholes that date back to the Bulge. They aren't as deep as they once were, but they are still there, 10- and 15-feet apart. They are not unlike the old men who come to visit here, diminished versions of their former selves. Amazingly, these holes where one or two men cowered, fought, died aren't protected by handrails or marked by interpretive signs. Nor is there a nearby kiosk selling trinkets. Nobody's trying to make a buck. We were the only ones here.

These woods were defended by US infantrymen including those of Easy Company[9] made famous in the HBO series *Band of Brothers*. Martin told my sons about German fragmentary mortars that exploded at treetop level. The shrapnel and splintered half of the tree would rain down in the pattern of an umbrella. The only safe place was to be huddled at the trunk of the hit tree. A one-legged American described this deadly debris pattern to Martin in that very wood; he had scrambled out of his foxhole and every part of his body except a leg had made it to the safe trunk of the tree.

Less than a mile north, in the village of Noville, Martin took us to an unassuming stone monument etched with the names of eight local men executed by the SS in retaliation for the village's earlier support for US troops. One of the executed men was Abbe Delvaux Louis, the local priest who offered his own life in order that a father of twelve be set free. Most who live in that village now are related to that spared man. Martin told our boys that all kinds of sacrifices were made in "your grandfather's war."

Our sons paid rapt attention, partly because Martin looked at each so fiercely in the eye, partly because the narrative enthralled them. This was no boring history lesson, nor were there many opportunities to doze. Stories, jokes, questions, silence. Martin used them all in the service of a perfect dramatic monologue. With his rolling brogue, he lauded all things Scottish—whiskey, language, and kilts, to name three. We laughed a lot.

Martin didn't hide his enthusiasm to be with us, nor his penchant for drawing history with flair. As he drove—we were heading south again to Bastogne three miles away—he described the weapons. The German Nebelwerfer delivered rockets from five- and six-tube launchers. Because the shells were thin and light, they could carry more explosive. Flying through the air, they made a terrifying sound—which Dad knew well—earning them the name screaming meemies. Martin spoke of the German armies that would blitz the Allied line on the morning of December 16; the SS north of Dad were the most feared. He talked about Hitler's desperate frame of mind at this point in the war. An attempt had been made on the Fuhrer's life in July. Erwin Rommel, the general linked to the failed conspiracy, was too popular among the German populace to execute, so he was invited to commit suicide, which he did by cyanide in October, about the time Dad arrived in Glasgow. Hitler had become insanely paranoid as his top secret Wacht Am Rhein (watch/guard on the Rhein) attack plans came together. He refused the counsel of his generals who maintained that such an attack in the

Ardennes wouldn't work. Though the offensive famously failed, it inflicted brutal damage, pushing back—or bulging— the allied line nearly to the Meuse River. In only 41 days, the allies suffered 89,987 total casualties: 19,276 dead, 47,493 wounded, 23,218 captured or missing.[10] German losses totaled over 80,000.

American troops, green to the front and untried in combat, were aware of German movements along the quiet front well before the attack began, but higher ups dismissed intelligence that indicated something was afoot. From London and Washington to the lowest grunt, most believed the war in Europe was soon over. Complacency had set in. As unlikely as a German attack on this front was, the thinking went, it wouldn't prove too serious. Never mind that 55 regiments of battle-tested soldiers were gearing up to crush the allied line of American GIs who missed their mothers' cooking and dreamed of girls or young wives back home. No doubt the Germans daydreamed about the same things.

Benjamin was crammed in the very back of the van where I would have been seasick in under 20 seconds. I was so grateful. I needed to remember to thank him. In the middle, behind where Martin and I sat in the front, Rachel, Joseph, and John Mark were strapped side by side like paratroopers.

Martin's eyes sparkled as he talked of interviewing Himmler's granddaughter; they narrowed and darkened when he mentioned trench warfare in WWI. The woods along the Schnee Eiffel where the German blitzkrieg was aimed have been harvested for lumber at least twice since WWII, he said. When I told him that I had read that they were firs, he said that perhaps was the case during the war. But loggers, he said, replanted with 'real' trees. "They're Scottish Pines now!" he bellowed, winking again.

Steam rose from the warm streets and light rain fell as we entered Bastogne. We jogged in for a quick tour of the Centre d'Interpretation Deuxieme Guerre Mondiale housed in the Heintz barracks—a Belgian army barracks—that served as the command center for the beleaguered 101st Airborne Division. The 101st had been hopelessly surrounded just days after the battle began, but instead of surrendering as the Germans demanded them to do, commanding General McAullife uttered his now-famous, one-word response: Nuts.

The basement rooms, affectionately called the Nuts Cellar, are small, and the ceiling low. Another small group of visitors wandered around solemnly. Displays of uniform-clad life-sized mannequins, battle maps, and radio gear were roped off, but that didn't stop Martin. He stepped over the rope in the first room we entered, grabbed a rifle and thrust it into John Mark's small hands.

"There," he said proudly. "Every lad needs to hold a Thompson submachine gun on his twelfth birthday." He crowned John Mark with a scarred captain's helmet.

John Mark began to laugh nervously, taking care not to drop the heavy gun and to keep the helmet on his head. The rest of us leaned back in the small room and began pulling out our cameras. Martin doled out a metal grease gun to Joseph then traded an M1 Garand for John Mark's Tommy gun. I recognized the M1 as the type of rifle Dad had been issued in basic training.

I hid silent behind my camera. I snapped picture after picture after picture. Framed in my camera—and perhaps forever in my brain—were these giggling, unlikely soldiers. In December 1944, my baby-faced Dad may have looked about as out of place as my young sons.

That John Mark was clutching an unloaded M1, his Pop's genes swimming through his trigger finger, wigged me out a little. Something rattled inside my head and hurt. As he turned around to look at his brothers, John Mark inadvertently jabbed the gun at the crotches and bellies of everybody else in the room. He had never handled a rifle before, a fact obvious to those in the room who winced and hopped when he pointed it at them. But he was wearing one of the biggest birthday grins I had ever seen, and for once my talkative child stood completely speechless. A beaming Joseph shuffled in place behind him, camera in one hand, grease gun awkwardly in the other. Benjamin clad in his blue Riverside Band hoodie leaned to one side, on guard for what Martin might pull next. A live grenade?

As my brand new 12-year-old locked into and out of focus on my camera screen, I felt a heaviness of heart. My sons couldn't know—and neither could I, really—what these very real weapons did to body and bone in the winter of 1944. After 40 minutes of poking through the exhibits and reading the interpretive wall plaques, we braved a steady shower of bracing rain for the van. "We're heading north, now," Martin reported. "To St. Vith. To where your dear father fought."

Dad sweated through basic training that summer in Fort Sill, Oklahoma, with J.P. On their first weekend leave, Dad reported sheepishly "they drank the town dry." Arrested, the revelers were corralled in the local jail, but not charged. These solemn drunks represented the fighting machine this country needed. Untold dollars had already been sunk into their training.

On another weekend, afraid of being AWOL, the young bucks flew through the night in a jeep, racing to get back to camp by morning. They crashed into a horse on the road. Its poor head demolished the windshield. "We were dead meat if we got caught," Dad reminisced. They didn't get caught, but when the bloody jeep and deceased equine were found, whose head rolled for that? It's hard to believe that somebody wasn't made to take the fall. If anybody did, it wasn't my dad.

J.P. and Dad were assigned to different units after basic. Their goodbye at Fort Sill wouldn't be their last, but they didn't know that then. So many of the men with whom they trained wouldn't live to see their twenty-first year.

Dad celebrated his twentieth birthday with the newly formed 106th division at Camp Jackson, South Carolina, just in time to climb aboard a truck convoy bound for Camp Atterbury, Indiana. He spent much of the spring and summer there training, waiting, training some more. Marksmanship, survival skills, field hygiene, weapons, navigation and communication, running, hand to hand combat, first aid, foot marches. Days in the field. Learning how to trust your equipment and skills. Little time off. Learning how to trust the men in your squad. Indy was 30 miles north on US 31. The town of Edinburgh was a long walk from the east gate. A burger, fries, and a milkshake would have been worth the walk. Schaffer Drugs on Main Street would have been able to set a young GI up with a plate. And the USO there would have had food, bands, and the softer, softer sex.

They pranked each other when off duty. They read old *Life* and *Time* magazines and watched Jean Arthur and Charles Coburn in Hollywood movies on Army-issued projectors. They were bored, worried, lonely. They stood around, polished boots, day dreamed. Sometimes they fought. They played catch. At 144 pounds, Dad would have been on the small side for tackle football. He still had not grown into his strong hands and wind-flap ears, but he was nimble and fast.

Some would have written long letters home. Soon after I left for college I got a postcard, one of only two or three personal notes my dad ever sent me. His cursive was neat, compact, and easy to read. His penmanship suggested there was nothing rushed or complex about the message or the writer; his cursive words were a few elegant, long waves at the beach when the whole ocean was smooth as glass. If Dad did write letters home in his war years, my Aunt Alice remembers only one: in early April 1945 the family got three words from Dad, written in pencil in that same, easy script, on an American Red Cross post card. It said, "I am fine." That was good news from a POW whom both the Army and the family feared was dead. He had said what was essential. He had written what folks back home hungered to hear.

Other guys may have scoured the *Indianapolis Star* for news about the war. They read about the invasion at the beaches of Normandy, the Allied push towards Paris while the Reds circled Mogilev and Orsha. They read about the bruising Hitler got in an assassination attempt that might have ended the war before men like my dad got there; they read about Roosevelt's nomination for a fourth term, Japanese losses in Saipan. Some read the sports pages. Dad wasn't a big reader. By the time I came along, light years after the war, his sports interests were limited to golf and tennis, and they were only lukewarm. His eyes lit up, however, at the prospect of making an acquaintance. He was more interested in—and good at—striking up conversation with the guys. Where are you from? Tell me about your home town. You got a girl back home? What does your old man do? Any kid brothers or sisters?

Home. A three-star flag hung in the front window of 68 Cherokee Road, Hampton, Virginia. Prayers ascended for him from the congregation at Hampton Baptist Church on Kings Way downtown. Mrs. Carrie Massenburg stood one Sunday, asking prayers for her son, shot down in Pacific. Dr. John H. Garber closed eyes obscured by bushy white eyebrows and prayed, but they never heard from Alvin again.

There was no girl waiting back home for Dad, per se, but many he would want to be remembered to. His father, a major by now in the Army Air Force, was a stateside camp inspector who was absent from home the whole war, hopping from camp to camp; at the time of his son's capture Joe Matthews was stationed at Godman Field, Kentucky. Nine-year-old Alice, the last of the litter in his family, held the home front with her mom and sister Angeline, when she wasn't away at Madison College in the valley; very pregnant Mary Louise was in Philly with her Navy husband; brother Jimmy, a commissioned lieutenant, was God only knows where in Europe in the artillery.

Dad may have asked, *When Uncle Sam lets us take off these itchy uniforms, what are you doing after the war?* But some questions might have been taboo. Talking about the future could jinx it. Dad wasn't superstitious, but he knew when to leave something alone, all the same. And didn't their training instill in them an attentiveness to the present? Infantry grunts didn't have to think, only to do. Enlisted men didn't pour over maps and make decisions. They didn't plan the war, only fought it. Dad never was one to make big plans for the future, anyway.

They whiled their time away playing cards. Dad's game was poker. His ability to intuit *and* calculate was a winning skill when he learned contract bridge after the war, but it also worked well enough for poker in Indiana. And because he didn't care much whether he won or lost, his winnings were usually lost before he had a chance to spend them. No matter. The army offered three free squares a day, and the free USO shows, the dancing, and the bands filled with old hipsters, four-eyes, flat-foots, and other talented deferments. Mainly, they trained and trained that summer, and went to bed tired, tried not to think about what was to come, and were kicked awake at zero-dark-thirty before sunrise, before they even had time to dream.

Summer raced into fall. More training. More waiting. In October they boarded trains for the two day trek to Camp Miles Standish, Massachusetts. Their waiting was almost over.

Joe Hilbers remembers getting a single evening pass to nearby Boston. "Not much happened," he recalls. There was a picture taken with some local girls; the print was lost in his abandoned duffle bag during the confused retreat during the Battle of the Bulge. "Only other thing I remember is that we ate at a very good restaurant and on a dare from a couple of Midwestern boys, who had serious reservations about oysters, I consumed a dozen oysters on the half shell at their expense."

The Old Howard Theatre had fallen into seedier days from its Shakespearian heyday, but offered up a spicy fare of burlesque affordable to all comers, as did the Casino Theatre and Crawford House. Dad would have loved window shopping the square, catching a fight or a show, roaming in and out, taking it all in, bar crawling with other men. The market price for the broiled whitefish was $1.25. Roasted prime rib was $1.85. A couple of hot dogs and a beer could be had for 70 cents. There's so much he never talked about; but how could he have forgotten the likes of Peaches, the star of the Casino who had "majestic buttocks" and specialized in what one old Navy salt remembers as *the shimmy*? On Sunday afternoon on October 22, the Boston Yanks were schooled by the Philadelphia Eagles 38-0. It was a windless, cool 53 degrees. That night the moon rose nearly full.

The men of the 106th, thrown together less than a year before at Fort Jackson and mixed with a constant influx of new and last minute replacements, were as trained as time would allow. The war wasn't waiting, and they needed to ship out and join in. At Camp Miles Standish they loaded into trains for their last ride stateside to the docks of Luxury Liner Row in Manhattan.

It didn't matter what Lorraine and Max Gordon were cooking up at the Village Vanguard jazz club down nearby Seventh Avenue. Nor did it matter that Arthur Rubinstein was playing Carnegie Hall, or that members of Glenn Miller's band were jamming at the USO. There was no time to catch a show. No time to slip away for a soda or a walk. There was no time for a collect telephone call home, even though he had the numbers memorized; home was 5882. Granny's was 6587. Uncle Paul's was 6202. All the training. All the waiting. Now there was a crushing rush to leave. The 106th was marched off trains and herded directly onto pier 84.

Martin took the curves slowly through the close streets of Houffalize. He told us about a trout stream that runs near the road, but Benjamin was dead asleep folded in the back, and the rest of us were glazed with jet lag and a day's ride. We were as quiet as a pond. Martin's small talk dribbled to silence, and I was left with images of this quaint town sliding serenely past. Germans and Americans carpet-bombed the town, reducing it to rubble. When Patton came through near Christmas of 1944, he was appalled by the utter destruction; he exploited a Christmas carol with this profane but true lyric:

O little town of Houffalize,
How still we see thee lie;
Above thy steep and battered streets
The aeroplanes still fly.
Yet in thy dark streets shineth
Not any Goddamned light;
The hopes and fears of all thy years
Were blown to hell last night.

Dad's 422nd defended about 9,000 yards of the thin frontline in the Ardennes forest. They had dug in along the eastern edge of the Schnee Eiffel, a pastoral, wooded ridge roughly marking the Belgian-German border. Dad was some six or more miles east of St. Vith, across the German border, near the tiny town of Schlausenbach. I deduced his location from battle histories and what little Dad told me: he was on the frontline, he was in the woods on a ridge, he was near St. Vith, and—he never failed to mention this fact—it was cold. At 80-some miles from a point near Luxemburg almost to Aachen, this battlefront was too wide for the thinly manned American troops to defend against a substantial attack. Until November, however, the German defenses were too anorexic to mount any substantial attack. In 1965, Hugh Marshall Cole, writing for the Office of the Chief of Military History of the U.S. Army, concluded that military professionals learned many lessons from the Battle of the Bulge regarding dispersal, gaps between units, counterattack doctrine, widths of front, and fluidity of movement.[11] Troops were dispersed too thinly, units were too far apart, the front was too wide, and—thanks to poor communication and green troops among other factors—troop movement was sluggish and ill-coordinated.

Immediately to the north of the 422nd, within hiking distance, around the Loshiem Gap, was the attached 14th Calvary. Immediately to Dad's south, again within hiking distance, was the 423rd based around Oberlascheid. Further south, around tiny Grosslangenfeld where the Eiffel curls eastward, was the 424th. These were the three regiments of the 106th division, which was headquartered to the west in the crossroads town of St. Vith.

Dad got to the front from the coast at Le Havre, jostled in the back of a canvas-covered deuce and a half for the 350-mile trek. No wonder he never could tell me much about his location. He didn't see much looking backwards out of a sluggish truck. One road looked like the next and every town was similar. When Dad was in Belgium, he had no guide as we did in Martin King. Nor were the roads clear. In the winter of 1944, the roads not oozing with mud were obscured by drifts of snow sometimes as high as fence posts.

The Brit George MacDonald Fraser fought the Japanese in Burma and wrote about it at the end of his life. "With all military histories it is necessary to remember that war is not a matter of maps with red and blue arrows and oblongs, but of weary, thirsty men with sore feet and aching shoulders wondering where they are."[12]

Dad did what he was ordered to do and went where he was directed to go, mainly by following the men in front of him. And what he remembered about his location? Front lines. In the woods. Near St. Vith. And *it was cold.*

"When I was in Europe," wrote Louie Andrews, Jr., my minister when I grew up, "I was 19-years-old, had no idea of command, or even at times where I was, even in what country. My memories are mostly good memories of being in France after the war in Europe ended. It seems I only really remember the bad parts in my dreams."

Dreams were a geography about which Dad never spoke.

Winding roads to the battle positions are still narrow, built not for tanks but for bicycles, horses and carts. A flatbed of hay, dwarfed by 68-ton Tiger tanks, was once considered a wide maximum load on those roads. But tanks plowed through these village lanes anyway. These rural capillaries were often blocked by traffic jams of every manner of vehicle and truck hauling weary soldiers. The blockages halted the advance of whole German divisions, driving the German generals mad with anger. The German battle plan depended upon surprise, which they achieved smashingly, and speed, which, thanks to the delaying actions of Allied units and clogged roads, they did not gain.

Dad had been dumped on the front six days before the fighting broke out. They had come to replace the Second Infantry Division who, when they left, took their heating stoves with them. Green troops went to this part of the line to get broken in, as did battle weary troops to rest and regroup. Some called it the Ghost Front, because it was so sparsely populated with troops from either side. The guys in the Second told the likes of my dad that this was a quiet sector. Welcome to Easy Street.

That's what the 106th desperately needed: time to get their act together without being shot at. Throughout the spring and summer of 1944 the U.S. Army had siphoned replacement troops from the 106th while they were still stateside. These replacements filled in wherever they were needed all across Europe. By the time Dad loaded into the RMS Aquitania (some of the 424th regiment came over in the Queen Mary), the 106th division had been picked over and then hastily reassembled. Half of the GI's were so new to the division they hadn't been thoroughly trained. Further, the 106th—formed only a year before—had no military history, no *esprit de corps*. The 106th, some say, was crippled at the start because they had not formed into a combat *team*. They fell short not only in experience, but as importantly, in the unity of other divisions.

Prior to our trip, at the beginning of my sabbatical, I met Hu Lacquement at one of my talks about my new novel *Mercy Creek*. Hu is a retired Army colonel. His father was a Methodist chaplain in the 14th Calvary, that unit just to the north of Dad at Loshiem. I told Hu about my dad saying that not only had he never once fired his weapon in battle, he hadn't even been issued ammunition. Dad was so new to the front, they never got around to him with his allotment of bullets.

Hu shook his head and said that was impossible. As an old quartermaster, his hackles might have been up. When soldiers are asked, "Did you kill anybody," a common answer, Hu said, was, "I fired my weapon in the direction of the enemy *a lot*." Hu suggested that Dad was trying to protect me; he didn't want his son to know he had killed people. Or, he just couldn't talk about it. Of all that my dad forgot, I can't believe he got this mixed up. Not having bullets in a war would be hard to forget.

Joe Hilbers from San Francisco *had* been issued bullets, and he hasn't forgotten the battle.[13] He was on the front lines with the 422nd. The *front* quickly became the *rear* as they were surrounded and ordered to turn around and engage the enemy on the Schönberg Road that ran into St. Vith. On December 18—the third day of battle—they camped in the woods. No tents, no fires, no smoking. In addition to his M1, Hilbers was carrying a bandolier of ammo for another man's Browning automatic rifle (BAR), three boxes of K rations, and two grenades. He had abandoned his barracks bag, which held the platoon football and the picture of the girls from Boston. On December 19 his squad took up battle formation at the rear as his company began moving up the ridge towards the road.

"The company almost immediately came under fire from German 88mm guns, mounted on tanks. This was the word passed down the line. When the artillery fire started it was directed to the men in front of us so we found a convenient creek bottom, that had cut deeply into the hillside, for cover. Then . . . almost before the attack could get started the men in front were moving up the hill with their hands up over their heads. We could hardly believe our eyes."

Before sunset, he and the others had surrendered.

Forty minutes into our curvy ride I began seeing road signs announcing our approach to St. Vith. Food would be good, a sandwich, something. I get easily car sick, and the curvy ride was close to doing me in. My growling stomach settled a bit as my friend Jim Burrows came to mind. A lieutenant in one of Patton's rifle platoons, he was in Houffalize and St. Vith on his way eventually to the Rhine after Christmas in 1944. Jim introduced me to the term "worm's-eye-view." That's what a grunt in the infantry had: the perspective of a worm. An infantryman saw or knew nothing except what was directly in front of him and under his boots. All Dad knew was the guy to his left and the guy to his right. Sixty years later, he didn't even remember that.

After getting sandwiches at Fonk's Backwaren on Hauptstrasse, we strolled back to the circle where Martin met us with the van. The sun had broken through. The muggy chill began to evaporate. I swung my brown paper bag with a foot-long egg and ham sandwich in it. I jammed a plastic bottle of Coke in my front pocket. Bright cerulean had replaced the slate sky. We reluctantly climbed back into the van. After only a few minutes of climbing higher and deeper in the woods, we pulled over and got out.

On top of the shaded ridge it was quiet and still. Hawks spiraled upward upon thermals from the sunshine colored fields sprawled below. I took a big bite of my sandwich. The boys had devoured theirs in the car; they were wandering beyond earshot. Rachel gave me some distance but kept me protectively in her peripheral vision. From our vantage in the cool shade under the pine, we had a stunning view of fields below, and of the windmills, barns, and clusters of trees. The hawks wound higher and higher into the blue.

After several minutes of silence, Martin whispered to me, "We're close, Matthew. We're really close."

I nodded. And I felt a passing closeness to history as many casual battlefield tourists have probably felt, as if other hearts were beating inside my own. The ground on which we stood was verily connected to the frozen ground that Dad could not successfully defend in the winter of 1944 and on which he would be ordered to surrender or face certain annihilation.

Is it impious or dishonorable to eat an egg-and-ham sandwich near where your father could have died? I took a few more hungry bites followed by a shot of Coke. The breeze felt so good, so brisk. I needed this: the solid earth, the fresh air, the sandwich. I tried to take this all in. Proximity. Transcendence. Had Dad and I come alone years before, we would never have found this ridge above the St. Vith-Schönberg Road by ourselves. And this isn't far from where Dad was trapped in war. I swallowed.

"Am I looking towards Germany?" I finally asked.

Martin touched my shoulder and turned me around. He pointed. "Now you are."

I swallowed again.

"We're close," Martin said to no one.

"Ah," I heard myself say. "So close. So close. So close."

Here the skies erupted at 5:30 on Saturday morning, December 16th. Screaming meemies shrieked overhead for an hour, tenderizing the Allied line behind Dad's forward position. German spotlights crisscrossed the leaden skies. Cold sabers of white light bristled off heavy clouds. Frozen shadows made trees loom and stagger. GIs hunkered down wondering what hell these Germans had unleashed. Dad said he pulled his helmet tight over his head and nearly lost his mind. The end of the world had come.

Dawn slowly brightened the dreary skies. As though some god had flicked a switch, the shelling stopped. Dad could hear motors rumbling before him and distant canon fire but could see nothing. My whole life I've wondered what it was like for him at that terrifying moment. Could he hear his belly rumble, blood swishing through veins, heavy breathing? Did he feel madness welling up inside? The sound of motors became more distant and the morning grew portentously silent.

He and others in his second battalion B company kept looking in the wrong direction, into Germany. That's where they expected the Germans would come. These troops were *volksgrenadiers*, Army divisions organized around battle-tested veterans and then bulked out with whatever the German populace had left to muster: wounded soldiers; leftovers from regular army, navy, and air force units; old men; teenagers. Highly patriotic to the Reich, they were ready to fight. Popping cautiously up and down from holes, American GIs kept looking toward the front, waiting for them. The air smelled of exploded earth, new snow, diesel. Fog draped the branches like tissue paper. Mist settled in the creases of the land along with the terrible, numbing cold.

The waiting was agony. Certainly more than one young GI entertained the possibility of a bullet shearing off his head onto his buddy's lap. His own head in a vise, Billy Boy didn't know the Fifth and Sixth Panzer armies had punched holes in the Allied line immediately to his north and south. Before the shelling began, Germans quietly slipped between Dad's 422nd and the 14th Cavalry a few clicks to the north; this was a particularly wide gap in the thin line. In the south, Germans sliced between dad's neighboring 423rd and 424th. Dad, in the calamitous middle, didn't know that a quarter of a million German soldiers[14] had streamed through the line above and below his formerly quiet position. Some 980 tanks rumbled eastward with experienced troops, supported by 2,000 cannons. He didn't know that the 18th Volksgrenadier Division marched through Weckerath, Roth, and Kobscheid—only two miles away.

Cloudy, cold, and drizzling snow and ice, it was what Patton called "Hitler weather" because the superior Allied air forces could offer little or no air support through such impenetrable skies. The GIs strained to peer through the muck. Mists were so thick that some German soldiers to the north crept right past Americans, and neither side saw the other.

I attempted many conversations with Dad about the battle. He said very little and I got very little. I wonder if to him my unceasing curiosities felt like death by a thousand paper cuts—over three decades. In the end, the word "confusion" was as clear as Dad could describe what was happening. He heard German motors and imagined equipment on the move, but could not guess where they were or where they were going. For their part, many Germans moving west thought the invisible Americans had retreated to the Our River a few miles behind the line to the west.[15] Dad didn't know that after daybreak on Saturday, Germans commanded the crossroads at Auw *behind* his position. Dad said he had no idea that he was becoming surrounded.

After the initial screaming barrage of Nebelwerfer rockets on Saturday morning, it was eerily quiet for Dad, but not for everyone. A half dozen miles to the south, the 62nd Volksgrenadier Division cut into the 424th at Heckhuscheid and Winterspelt. Back to the north, by 8:30 a.m., a German tank in Roth belted a US command post with direct fire. American light tanks from Manderfield—no contest for the larger, better armored Panzer and Tiger tanks—rushed to give aid, but were stopped cold by fire from Auw.

By 9:00 a.m., Kobsheid fell.

By noon, Germans in Auw moved south penetrating the northern and rear flank of the 422nd, whose HQ in Schlausenbach was endangered.

By 1:30 in the afternoon, the commander of the 422nd, Colonel George L. Descheneaux, who was commissioned a colonel at the age of 32, sought to support the artillery being targeted by Germans. It was heavily snowing now. Nearly immediately, Descheneaux was forced to turn around to defend Schlausenbach.

By late afternoon, the 14th Cav had become separated from the north flank of 422nd leaving both regiments exposed. By dark, in the south, Germans had closed in on Winterspelt. By midnight, they had captured it.

On this first day of battle, Dad saw no action. He and others in the 422nd simply held their positions and waited, for what they did not know.

On the second day of battle, by 5:30 on Sunday morning, Germans had taken, lost, and retaken Bleialf, south of Dad's position. Next, the Americans abandoned Schönberg immediately to Dad's west. By 9:05 a.m., German troops pushing up from Bleialf met the German troops streaming down from Auw at Schönberg. They took the villages and the crossroads. The noose was complete. The 422nd and 423rd were completely surrounded, trapped in *der kessel*— the pocket—pinned against the western slope of the Eifel. Reports vary, but some seven to nine thousand Americans were bottled up in the western folds of the wooded ridge of the Schnee Eifel.[16]

The shelling and German scouts behind the lines shattered communication. Radio communication from regiment to regiment, and back and forth to headquarters made only sporadic connections. Many communications were not received, or incompletely received, or delayed. Some were misunderstood. The radio order from St. Vith at 9:45 a.m. for the 422nd and 423rd to "withdraw from present positions if they become untenable" was delayed in transit, and would have been received too late to obey even if it had arrived 12 hours earlier. On the whole the Americans of the 422nd and 423rd were left alone while German infantry, guns, and vehicles muscled past on their way west.[17]

By Sunday evening, the 422nd set up a tightened perimeter around Schlausenbach. To the south, three miles away, the 423rd did the same on the high ground around Oberlascheid and Buchet. The 422nd had one day's K-rations at hand. They were running out of surgical supplies. Kitchen trucks had been lost, but only forty wounded men were reported for evacuation for the 422nd. The 423rd wasn't so lucky: 225 KIA, MIA, or wounded.

Reinforcements were promised but never came. Even had clogged roads and sluggish movement and communication allowed it, they would have had to break through armored columns of Germans to get to the entrapped American units. The 422nd and 423rd were well behind the front line as it bulged west. Dad and others waited anyway—not only for reinforcements of fighting men and armor, but also for air drops of medical supplies and food. None of it came, hampered by appalling communication and German penetration beyond Allied knowledge. Inexperienced higher ups in the back couldn't comprehend the tremendous velocity or volume of German resources being thrown into this "quiet sector," nor did they act quickly enough to salvage better results.

On day three, at 2:15 Monday morning, General Jones (who would be relieved of command by Friday) ordered the 422nd and 423rd to head to Eimerscheid-Schönberg-St Vith road to head off a Panzer regiment. The effort could not be coordinated because both regiments had lost radio contact with each other. Out numbered, out gunned, and completely surrounded, the Americans were in an untenable situation but just didn't know it yet.

The 423rd destroyed its kitchens and excess equipment, left the wounded with medical aid men in the regimental collecting station, and headed to the road anyway. By 11:30 a.m. Colonel Puett's 2nd Battalion of the 423rd encountered Germans near the Schönberg-Bleialf road. Thirty minutes later, he sent an urgent plea for help. None came. Puett dug in at Ihren Creek, 1,000 to 1,500 yards from edge of Schönberg.

Dusk on Monday brought even more confusion. The 1st Battalion of the 423rd put in on the left of the 2nd to help clean the German infantry from the shadowy woods astride the Bleialf-Schönberg road. Meanwhile, men from 422nd thought they were in an assembly area in a wood near Schönberg; they were actually lost at the edge of Oberlascheid. By nightfall on Monday, all attempts from Colonel Cavender of the 423rd to reach their 422nd sister regiment had failed. And 423rd casualties were high: 300 men, including 16 officers. No rounds remained for 81-mm mortars. Most machine guns were gone. Rifle clips were low. The 423rd had pulled itself together in some semblance of order along Ridge 536, just southeast of Schönberg. Much of the 422nd was just south of Laudesfeld. Dad, of course, had no idea where he was—like a perfect pearl lost in snow.

The thrust of the German attack had punched well towards the west, despite valiant delaying actions by scrambling American troops. These delaying actions made a huge difference. Their timetable thrown off, Hitler's troops would remain mired in the Ardennes. Neither German tanks nor men would ever capitalize upon the flatter land and better roads along the Meuse River.

One hour after dawn on Tuesday, December 19th (the fourth day of the battle and 74 hours during which the Americans had gotten no significant sleep), German field pieces along the Bleialf-Schönberg road opened fire, sweeping the slope of a ridge battle maps identify as number 536. Men were shredded. Around two o'clock in the afternoon, mistaking the movement of the 423rd for enemy, the 422nd poured fire into them, wreaking even more chaos on these men wasted by hunger and battle fatigue. For those not already dead, this would be their last day of fighting in WWII. They would soon taste their own death, or—as most did—surrender.

Dad remembered the cold, the cold, the cold. "Snow falling and night falling fast, oh, fast," wrote Robert Frost in 1936.[18] Dad remembered the snow, the cold, and the excruciating, long nights. To the south, in Bastogne, it was 14-degrees Fahrenheit. Francis "Bud" Street remembered the macadam road to Bastogne was a "mud pit."[19]

Late Tuesday afternoon, a vehicular column of Americans attempted to break out to the west through Bleialf, to the south but were stopped by a mine field at the edge of the village. They were surrounded, and surrendered.

In the north, just after two o'clock, German tanks rolled in and took aim on many of the 422nd. German infantry seethed into the woods. "My God," Colonel Descheneaux is reported to have said, "we're being slaughtered." Final radio transmissions were made. NEED AMMO. FOOD. WATER. And, WE ARE NOW DESTROYING OUR EQUIPMENT. A half hour later, Descheneaux decided to do what some deemed the unthinkable. "I don't give a damn if I'm court-martialed," he said about his decision to surrender. At about the same time, Colonel Cavendar of the 423rd reached the same conclusion. By four o'clock Tuesday afternoon, December 19th, after negotiations ensuring that the Germans would feed the Americans and care for the wounded, surrender was complete. The battle had begun only 82-hours before, and now it was finished. The 422nd, 423rd, and fragments of their attached and supporting units became prisoners of war—an altogether different hell.[20] Dad was one of them.

Dad headed east while German armored units and tanks lurched west on narrow roads from one traffic clog to another. The carnage begun on the weekend of December 16th continued. Germans executed 84 unarmed American soldiers on Sunday in a field near Malmedy. That same day in Wereth eleven black Americans who had surrendered were gunned down.[21] Gestapo shot Belgian civilians in Noville and Stavelot. The day after Dad's capture—Wednesday—Bastogne was besieged. St. Vith fell on Thursday; allied bombs reduced it to rubble by Christmas day. In January, Americans would execute unarmed German soldiers in Chenogne. Germans continued blasting their way west, hoping to take the Meuse and Liège. Their eyes were set on Antwerp, hoping to divide the Allied armies—separating Eisenhower in the south from Montgomery in the north—to force a negotiated peace.

German armies killed and bled as they trudged west, but after just four days of battle in which Dad never admitted to firing a single shot, he was facing east toward Germany. There was nothing for him to be confused about anymore. He was a prisoner of war. His captors confiscated his cigarettes and marched him and the other POWs through snow-draped hills toward railroad boxcars. It was a 25-mile hike to Gerolstein.

I used to ask Dad if he remembered any of the men with whom he fought. Except for the likes of J.P. Dale in basic, he did not. What did he remember of Belgium? Did he remember any road names, landmarks, towns? Did he see views like I was seeing right now?

He could pull very little from this murky, unvisited corner of his past. The cold made a lasting impression—the cold, the violence, the noise. There is much he might have remembered that he could not tell me, could not tell anyone because he simply dare not let it out. Ever. The expression on other men's faces may have been beyond his ability to describe. These pictures etched in his mind may have been worth tens of thousands of words no single one of which his lips could form.

The landscape was pretty, he'd say. It was snowy and cold. Very cold. St. Vith sounded familiar. In later years, when I was able to question more gently, I gently pushed. "What do you remember about St. Vith?"

"It was cold," he said. He always mentioned the cold. "We were trying to get back to the St. Vith road."

"Did you make it?"

Pause.

"No."

Pause again. He tried to reach back.

"Why didn't your make it to the St. Vith road?"

He looked at me like he was frightened. I didn't want to push, but gently, I did.

"Because," he blurted, exasperated. *"The Germans were in the way."*

Yes. The Germans.

"What else, Dad?"

He got quiet. He spoke of the morning it began, the sixteenth. That noise before daybreak had gotten to him, the Nebelwerfers particularly. He flinched when he spoke about it. The squeal of screaming meemies and the concussion of cannon fire pierced him still nearly 60 years later.

I let the silence fill the space between us, the silence that had been his ally through decades.

"What about your capture?" I asked. "What was that like?"

"We were ordered to get rid of our weapons," he said. "Not all of them did; some tried to make it out."

"Did they make it out?"

"Not that I know of."

I remained silent, and he continued.

"I remember taking apart my rifle and throwing the pieces in a creek."

He looked away, as he always did when he spoke of the war, and I noticed his hands were speaking an infantryman's sign language busy disassembling an imaginary M-1 rifle by rote. He could do it in his sleep in basic training, and, lo, these many years later the muscle memory remained.

"I just threw the pieces in the water."

The creek was possibly Ihren Creek. He tossed the pieces into the water. The trigger housing made a splash and sank. Then the operating spring. Did he have gloves? Surely he had gloves in that cold. Were his hands shaking with cold? With nerves? Were they steady enough to extract the hammer pin, the bolt?

"I carried a snapshot of Daddy."

By now his blue eyes were swimming. My white-headed father explained that *his* white-headed father was a major back in the states.

"I tore it apart and I threw it in the creek."

The paper shreds churned under the frigid water and were swept away. He chucked what was left of his rifle in the water.

I understood breaking down the gun. It was an order. The guns and ammo would be confiscated, used for more butchering. But the photograph?

"Why did you tear up the photo of your dad?"

"I didn't want it to be used against me," he said matter of factly. "I didn't want the Germans to know my father was an officer."

And maybe Dad didn't want the Germans to capture any more of him than possible. Tearing up that snapshot was a way of defending his father, protecting him from the horrors my father could neither imagine nor avoid. At least the Germans would never possess a photo of Dad's dad; they'd have Dad's name, rank, and serial number. That's all. But they wouldn't get my father's father, too.

Those pieces of metal and wood would never be reassembled. And that picture was gone for good, too. Neither would be used against my dad. But the memory of both remained.

"Then what?"

My words startled him. He was in another world.

"Dad, what happened next?"

He came to, looked me in the face, and said, simple as pie, "We put up our arms. We walked up the hill. And we surrendered."

"The distance between us and the immeasurable," wrote Richard Chess, "is no more than the distance between two rooms, even if the wall is a heaving ocean."[22] That's how close my father and I were for much of our relationship, but particularly at that moment.

Of all the things Dad forgot or never bothered to remember in the first place, his surrender wasn't one of them. He never forgot it. Part of him must have remained beside that winter creek in the bitter, Belgian woods. Thank God that most of him came home.

If midnight is a place, for my father, this was it.

5

Manhood

We left that ridge, bright with sun and somber with history, and drove through the tiny town of Schönberg towards the Losheim Gap thirty minutes northeast. This winding drive on narrow roads more or less paralleled the Allied line before German tanks and armor churned it to pieces on December 16. We rode silently and were not much more talkative when we stopped and stepped from the van. Here at the German border, we strolled down a rutted dirt road cut alongside wooden fence posts strung with barbed wire. Rows of concrete dragons' teeth—triangular blocks of concrete—protruded from the ground. Obscured by moss, German armor found passage around these anti-tank obstacles as they forced through between the 14th Calvary to the north and Dad's 422nd just to the south. Wind coursed through green fields of high grass and wild Queen Anne's Lace. Sandburg's war poem *Grass* came to mind:

Pile the bodies high at Austerlitz and Waterloo.
Shovel them under and let me work—
I am the grass; I cover all.

Thoroughly and beautifully the grass did just that in these empty, rolling pastures on that mild June day.

In 1944 a snarled traffic jam of Panzer divisions of the German Sixth Army inched westward in hopes of ultimately capturing Antwerp. A 29-year-old SS Storm Leader named Joachim Peiper rallied 4,800 men and 600 vehicles to Honsfeld where they captured the town and 50,000 gallons of Allied gasoline. Fourteen miles west, Kampfgruppe Peiper rolled into Malmedy on the second day of battle and machine-gunned some 90 American POWs who were assembled unarmed in a field blanketed with snow at the town crossroads.

Malmedy was our final stop. Martin took us there to stand in that executioner's field. After the Americans were mowed down, SS officers walked through the carnage asking who needed a medic; those who moaned were shot in the head at close range. Autopsies confirmed this grisly fact. Most of the frozen, snow-covered bodies weren't found until almost a month later. Some were hidden until April. There is no evidence at this lightly traveled crossroad of such violence now, of course. The grass has performed its perfect transformation here, too.

Across the street, a rock wall is a memorial to the slain, their names carved in stone inked in gold: Jones, Lucas, Davis, Perkowski. Roses, maintained by a grower in Tyler, Texas, bloomed in a large, raised flowerbed framed by railroad ties in the shape of a five-pointed star. We wandered around with our hands in our pockets. Our internal clocks hadn't adjusted yet, so we were tired, but I think we were wearied from Martin's account of all the carnage. I felt stunned. It was difficult to imagine the mad scramble of armies through these country lanes and unassuming villages and even harder to comprehend the depravity of war.

By now, the boys looked catatonic, and I think they were unable to take in any more of Martin's battle statistics and anecdotes. I found a way to touch each son as we walked along the wall and garden. Only a bodily connection would do; that's how transient the place made me feel. I bumped solidly into John Mark. I punched Joseph's shoulder. I put my arm around Benjamin. I wanted to close any space between us. I sought to forestall the separation that awaits all fathers and sons. With Joseph heading off to college in a month and the others not far behind, their scattering would happen soon enough, but not on this day. Today, far from home, we were one. I held Rachel's hand on our walk back to the van and kept watch over the boys racing to manhood. We were silent during the 40-minute drive back to Liège.

Growing up, I was afraid I'd have to do what Dad did in the war. As a young adult, I was afraid I wouldn't. "We've all felt that way, I'm confident," wrote Richard Ford in *The Sportswriter*, "since there's no way that I could feel what hundreds of millions of other citizens haven't."

I felt guilt. When I compared my life with Dad's I felt guilty for having it so good. And I did have it easy. Dad did not. When I was twenty, I struggled with statistics 101 and the difficulties of dating a gorgeous girl who lived ninety long minutes away. Dad had beriberi and nearly starved to death. As a Virginia Commonwealth University sophomore I struggled with the feelings that I had not met some ill-defined standard of true adulthood, which boiled down to one preposterous question: Is war the only passage to real manhood?

The "real" men in my life were the cowboys who always beat the Indians. They wore the white hats, out-drawing, out-shooting, out-smarting the black hats. They could land a flurry of impossible punches without breaking a sweat. Humphrey Bogart, not known for his westerns, could convey a real man's stance with just a look. *Gunsmoke*'s Matt Dillon was brave and resolute with a lot of firepower strapped around his waist. Paul Newman, Steve McQueen, and Robert Redford raced cars, hit homeruns, and got the pretty girls. There were the Pittsburgh Steelers' Iron Curtain. GI Joe. Hercules. Jimmy Connors and his intimidating serve and volley with a tennis racquet made of shining metal. A bare-chested Joe Namath cooling off with a splash of aftershave. There was David busting Goliath's chops, Moses staring down Pharaoh, Joshua knocking down walls. Even Sheriff Andy Griffith, who gave a gentler take on the male archetype, had a pistol-waving deputy and carried in his pocket the key to a whole rack of shotguns back at the jail.

And there was Bill Matthews. While my friends' dads were pretty cool, none had fought a war. Mine had, so in my elementary years some of the awe my friends accorded to my dad rubbed off on me. I was macho by association.

As a young teen, I understood that being a man meant bringing home the bacon, propagating the species, and, of course, fighting the wars. I looked forward to having a job, and I couldn't wait to do my part in making babies. But could I defend the borders? Would I be able to lock and load? My adolescent confusion over bravado and bravery was as embarrassing to me as acne. Was I worthy of the helpless but busty heroine if I wasn't willing to use my hands as lethal weapons?

Rev. Andrews was part of the problem. He was my much-loved minister at the small Presbyterian church of my youth. I took more seriously than most kids what my pastor said about peace. My take-away from long Sunday evening youth group conversations was that when Jesus said love your enemies he probably meant that we shouldn't kill them. The gospel according to John and the latest Bruce Springsteen albums—both of which my youth group thoughtfully parsed on Sunday nights—provided food for thought. Or fodder. Rev. Andrews was a WWII vet, and he sent a grown son to peacetime Korea, so his peace-loving point of view carried more weight than mere armchair peaceniks. He had walked the talk. And when he talked, I listened. He had been in the trenches as a soldier and agonized as the parent of a soldier. He tended towards pacifism but was no patsy. As a high school baseball ump, if he called you out at the plate, he did it in such a way that you didn't argue.

I'm not sure if Rev. Andrews was naïve in his understanding of justice and peace, or prophetic. But the glimpses of manhood I saw through his eyes made sense to me.

Usually I dozed during his sermons. But one I will never forget. He said that Jesus loved the world this much; Rev. Andrews stood before us with his arms stretched out wide.

Holding that posture, he said, "Jesus loved the world so much that he stretched out his arms," and looking to the cross on the wall behind him, he added, "and he died."

That moment still haunts me.

Service. Submission. Sacrifice. Discipleship. Rev. Andrews ambushed us with words like that in his preaching. He aimed them at us like flash coated nails from a nail gun. On that sleepy Sunday morning I began if not to understand than to appreciate this upside down, backwards view of what it meant to conquer. Turning the other cheek was defiance, not masochism and certainly not weakness. Walking the second mile. Giving the shirt as well as the coat. His word for it was "grace." I was beginning to discern that I had something to live for, and, if necessary, to die for.

This theology of service began to emerge as a new, as yet unreliable, definition of manhood. I was beginning to believe that extending kindness in a culture of hate and anxiety was as manly as laying down a cover of machine gun fire. This shift from muscles, brawn, and cigars was seismic. I was giving birth to a new world-view, and was seized in labor pangs. Rev. Andrews may have been the midwife, but I had to do the work of labor by myself. And it was *hard*. I remember as a teen and young man sometimes feeling so alone.

The world will ask those same sorts of questions of my boys. Does their *manhood* résumé measure up? The culture will try to tie their manhood to what they do, not to who they are. Will they be origami artists or Formula One drivers? Poets or weightlifters? I want my kids to know that bravery and bravado are different, the latter a sign of weakness and fear. Let them relish the men they are, even if they never kill a hog with a knife, or copter off to some distant war.

Bogart had a lot of swagger. At 5'8" he was bigger than life on screen, a tough guy with that slight lisp. "The only thing you owe the public," he's alleged to have said, "is a good performance." That may be true for actors, but not for the rest of us. We owe it to ourselves—much less *the public*—to be authentic. We owe it to ourselves to be ourselves. I want my boys to have balls and grace enough to be their own people, live their own dreams, be their own men. And God bless them if they don't fit into this week's fickle version of what manhood looks like.

I revisited these thoughts, flipping through them like well-worn flashcards as Martin sped through the late afternoon for our hotel in Liège. Rachel and the boys dozed. Those familiar inadequacies of my adolescence tumbled together *still,* like a pocketful of stones rubbed smooth by decades of distracted attention.

6

Almost Lost in Translation

We said goodbye to Martin at the curb of our hotel, and spent the next day in Liège decompressing. The combination of the flight and the eight hours traipsing through the battlefield left me numb, emotionally and otherwise. I needed some unprogrammed time to let the Belgian countryside sink in. I reminded myself that we were here to have fun, to *chillax* as my boys might call it. I was not supposed to brood the whole trip about loss, the frailty of fatherhood, human vanity, my father's apparent vow of silence about the war, and world peace.

We huffed up the steep hill behind our urban hotel and hiked the close side streets and hairpin turns taking pictures of pigeons, churches, and each other. Scaffolding encased the Basilica Saint Martin like a birdcage. The chapel around the nave was wrecked with construction. A pamphlet I picked up reported that St. Martin is the patron saint of war. What does the patron saint of war *do*, I wondered. Constantly weep? What can the inside of this white church teach me about the patron saint of war? To my family's chagrin, I grabbed the brass handles and yanked hard at the basilica's heavy, tightly locked doors. If churches are to be places of hospitality and sanctuary in life's tumult, we probably should stop locking them. What does this patron saint of war have to hide? I imagined a codebook of top secret prayers, indexed to include both the attackers and the attacked.

The boys and Rachel were enjoying themselves, talking wildly with their hands, and weaving down the sidewalk briskly away from me. I grabbed the door handles for another robust tug. No luck. I didn't want to leave, but stepped away from the church anyway, and started down the hill into town. I caught up with my family at Rue Mère Dieli in the direction of the Montagne de Bueren—a stone staircase rising 373 steps to the Citadel, an old fort whose crumbling walls stand on over 200 acres perched above the city. Though the map indicated we were close, we could not find the steps. Liège held us deeply in the palm of her hand, with buildings crowding close to narrow roads.

Then we saw it. Like a surgical incision through the neighborhood, the steps rose up and up in a zippered straight line through gardens, between apartments, and above a school playground. Stunned, we stood together at the bottom step taking in its height, the insane number of steps, and the anticipated energy required to ascend 20-plus stories through open air with only a single steel handrail to steady our nervous steps. Led Zeppelin may have been standing at this very spot when they became possessed with the idea of writing a song about climbing a stairway to heaven. After a moment, the boys launched for the top. Rachel and I began at something less than a gallop. The steps were built in 1881 to allow soldiers from the fort easier direct access to the city. Rachel didn't look down as she is nervous about heights. I wondered if she'd have the stomach for the long walk straight down. I'm famously nervous about heights, too, but I just pretended I was walking up an ordinary flight of stairs, from the first floor to the second, not from Liège to the moon. And I didn't look down, either. Our boys flew up like sparrows, their yelling spilling behind them like song.

Some 600 soldiers from Franchimont climbed the hill— without steps—in 1468 to take the camp of Charles the Bold,

Duke of Burgundy. Charles was also known as Charles the Rash and, to his enemies, Charles the Terrible. To his parents, Philip the Good and Isabel of Portugal, he was called Charles Martin. Charles took three wives. His first was the daughter of the King of France, Catherine. She was an older woman, by five years. On their wedding day in 1440, he was seven-years-old.

Angry that Charles had captured Liège, the Franchimontese wanted it back. Led by the Liège patriot Bueren, all 600 men were slaughtered, possibly because they were too tired to fight after the extraordinary ascent. Charles' troops plundered Liège for seven weeks.

The view didn't disappoint us after we crept up the last, brutal steps to the top. The rooftops of Liège, slated and slanting in every direction, struck me because of the tricks the angles played with mid-morning light. The lead-colored Meuse River meandered through the center of town. The river is navigable and eventually merges with other rivers to empty into the North Sea some one hundred miles down stream. Nothing about the Meuse causes me to want to swim, but I could have sat on that mountain and looked at it all day long. Those 373 steps were cause to sit and rest.

At the edge of the Citadel grounds stands a stone obelisk memorializing those who died in the First and the Second World Wars. I was ready to move beyond monuments to war dead, but I chided myself. These wars weren't "over there" like they were for folk in the United States. They were right here. Military veterans and their children walk every street here. Civilian survivors ride every bus, clerk every store, fill every factory.

Dad could seal off the war more easily than vets here, I imagined. At home not every person he met had been in the war, or had lost someone, or had been bombed or otherwise paid a price beyond rationing. Not so in Liège, or elsewhere in Europe.

Rachel went off with the boys along the old brick walls. I walked away from the great view of the city, away from monuments and thoughts of war dead. A bus driver circled his tour bus, kicking the tires. We struck up a conversation.

His English was better than mine. It was a lovely day, cool in the shade, breezy, bright beyond the trees.

His bus load of school children were out with their teachers exploring the fort. A retired Dutch cop, he proudly showed me his ID. The tiny picture matched the man before me wearing a robust smile and a thick head of short, white hair that still had some strawberry blonde in it. Reading glasses on a string hung across his chest. He wore a green striped necktie. I didn't have anything to show him except my passport, but that was hidden in the secret pouch attached by my belt and hanging so far down the inside leg of my pants that I would have had to strip to show it to him. This easygoing man drives two days a week as part of what he called "a great retirement."

Eventually the conversation turned to me, where I was from, and what I was doing here. He listened intently as I told the abbreviated story of my dad's capture in the Bulge.

"Yep," he said. "The war touched everybody."

In Holland, his grandfather was executed by Germans for harboring Jews on his farm. In the 1960s he'd been in the Dutch Merchant Marine. He told me about war games he had been part of with US Marines attached to the *USS Guadalcanal*. The Dutch played the role of the Vietcong. They were supposed to hide. The Americans were supposed to find and destroy them. It was a happy memory for him. Those were the days.

He had settled his trim, tall frame comfortably into his driver's seat. I stood on the shaded road leaning against the wide open door. A cool breeze brushed over my bare legs into the bus that smelled like new fabric. Reaching for his hand I thanked him for the visit. He clasped mine with both of his and wished me luck. I walked across the empty road with some hope of eventually finding my family. I was in no hurry to rush the graces of this delightful, cool morning.

Englishman Francis Ledwidge was killed in action in 1917. He wrote in his *Soliloquy* that "A keen-edged sword, a soldier's heart/ Is greater than a poet's art. And greater than a poet's fame/ A little grave that has no name." How many people—both soldiers and the citizens we've come to call *collateral damage*—were killed at this and other forts over the centuries, and then were hastily buried beneath nameless markers? Lincoln was right when he said at Gettysburg that we cannot hallow ground that has already run red. Such is not for us to do. But that doesn't stop us from trying with etched monuments like the one keeping vigil over Liège. "It is well that war is so terrible," Robert E. Lee is said to have uttered, "lest we should grow too fond of it." These words mock us.

By lunchtime, the boys were fading fast, particularly Joseph and Benjamin. Teenage boys eat inordinate amounts of food. Our stomachs growling, we walked to the end of a sunny side street—Rue Saint Georges— and found ourselves on the patio of a *ristorante* called Il Baro. Opting for the dark and cool of the modest indoors, we wound through sun-warmed, outdoor tables, and filed inside to a long table by a row of windows with clear panes of wavy glass. The boys plunked themselves heavily down into solid wooden chairs. Ben laid his head down on the solid table with an even more solid thud. He sighed deeply. Joseph perked up when the dark headed waitress in the tight apron brought us a few bottles of water; we poured the cold water with a flourish into glasses, clicked them ceremoniously, and gulped it down delicately like a tour group of Great Danes from the States. We emptied the bottles twice before we ordered and four more times before we declined dessert.

Besides the water, which I hoped was on the house, I ordered myself and Joseph a beer; he grimaced through a quarter of his bottle of Moretti while awaiting for the arrival of our lunch. Because it was so cold and so good and such a shame that most of his would go to waste, I took the sweating bottle off his hands after I quickly drained mine. I rather enjoyed the idea that Joseph's first legal swallow of beer (the legal age here I presumed was 18, not 21) required an international effort: the Italian beer was distributed by the good Dutch people at *Heineken* and served by a fine looking, French speaking waitress in a Belgian town.

We were well-hydrated but nearly ravenous when our meal came. I set about attempting to consume a calzone the size of an American football. The boys devoured several aromatic pizzas, then scarfed up Rachel's leftover pizza bones and the ends of my demolished calzone.

If they needed sleep before the heavy meal, they definitely needed eons of it now; unfortunately for them, a nap was out of the question until we made at least a cursory trip through the Museum of Walloon Art across the street. Begrudgingly, they followed me through its front doors.

As instructed, we took the elevator to the top floor. The galleries featuring art from the French-speaking areas of Belgium are designed in a walking circuit from the fifth to the ground floors, from the oldest to the most modern. We all began together with art from the Flemish Renaissance: Lombard, Paterier and Bles. Almost immediately, Joseph and Benjamin peeled off in a speed-walk. Rachel and John Mark moved at a leisurely pace, quietly talking about the sculptures of Leon Mignon and Felix Roulin.

I was glad to explore alone. I needed time for the images to sink in. I wondered what Anto Carte had in mind with his picture of the archers of St. Sebastian. They are stepping back to regard their handiwork. Sebastian—the patron saint of soldiers, the plague-stricken, and athletes—looks to have suffered six painful, largely non-lethal wounds. The goonish archers, nevertheless, seem pleased with their keen aim. Did Carte intend me to laugh at this picture or lament the senselessness of the carnage? Is sarcasm or political protest at work here? I don't know if this painting venerates the saint, the executioners, or nobody. Was Carte commenting about how people as ordinary as working class archers give in to do the horrible deeds for the powers of the state? I wasn't sure what was more difficult: pulling myself up the Montagne de Bueren or getting my head around this picture.

Halfway through the museum, I discovered I needed to use the restroom. The lobby restroom had no toilet paper. This gave the man at the welcome counter and me a reason to try a conversation. I would have preferred a variety of other topics, but this matter was pressing. Pointing in the direction of the first floor restroom, I said something like, "You have no toilet paper." I put my best French accent on the word *toilet*. I was rather proud of the way it sounded.

He leaned forward in his metal chair and gave me a polite but blank look.

I said again, *"Toilet paper."* On this go, I used outstandingly heavy accents on both words—like a Steve Martin version of Inspector Clouseau—*tio.let pa.per*. The man leaned further forward in his chair. He nodded. I could tell he wanted to be helpful, but he didn't have a clue about paper toilets. This was an art museum, after all, and I could have been making an oblique Andy Warhol reference.

To make matters worse for me, Benjamin and Joseph had completed their flash-tour and were sitting on the brown couch in the lobby watching me. This embarrassed me a bit, but necessity is the mother of invention and the grandmother of desperation, so I pressed on intrepidly through my vocabulary conundrum. The boys glared at me. I was pretty sure I could read their minds. I was a teenager once. *There he is. Embarrassing us again.*

"Toilet paper," I reiterated, impaling the clerk with my best accent of his native tongue. Hope may have been draining from my face. He looked perplexed but sympathetic, like Anto Carte's archers who look uncertain about what to do next. Six arrows are not enough? His narrowed eyes indicated that he was straining to understand me; but understanding seemed as if it would never come. Words had just fallen too short, so I did what I knew he could not mistake. Using my best mime, I held up my hand and with a modest flourish wiped my buttocks. I said it again: "Toilet paper."

The man's eyes widened immediately. He jumped, scurried to a closet, and emerged with three rolls of what I required.

"Voilà" he offered.

"Bingo," I responded. I wanted to give him a high five, but sudden movement might have led to disaster.

We both were grinning—he because the mystery was solved, me because relief was only seconds away. The connection had been made, barriers had been surmounted, the vast ocean and quarter of a continent had been spanned. Our cultures might be worlds apart in some aspects, like language, but in most we are the same. The basics are basically the same. My sons may have been embarrassed. Their old man did it *again*. The man at the counter, however, still wore a smile. He and I were true brothers. A friend in need is a friend indeed, my dad might have said, and the hospitable clerk had valiantly come through. It was like passing the peace in church: no grudges, no regret, only grace and a fleeting few seconds of heaven on earth. *All because of a toilet paper emergency.* I hoped my boys noticed.

After using the restroom, I resumed my self-guided tour. The translation problems posed by Delvaux and Magritte and their take on life, politics, and whimsy were no trickier than those grappled with at the front desk. Getting lost in translation is obviously nothing new. Just ask any surrealist.

Upon leaving the museum, my family thanked the kind man at the counter, *mercies* and *au reviors* all around. As they ambled out onto the plaza, the man asked me in a tentative English riddled with alien diphthongs, "Where are you from?" His English was atrocious, and he knew it, which is why I think it took real courage for him to ask. Our sign language exchange earlier had, perhaps, lowered his inhibition. We had been through a lot together, after all.

"The U.S.A." I said, *as if he couldn't tell.*

"Ah," he said. "Cali-for-nee-ay?"

"No," I said, chuckling a little. "South Carolina."

I wanted to tell him about my home, beginning with my ancestor John Parramore arriving from England on the *Bonaventure* to Jamestown in 1622. My people and this friendly clerk's family might have known each other long ago when they lived on the same continent. His distant cousins and mine may have been clerks in the London Company responsible for funding voyages to the Colonies. I wanted to invite him to visit the Upstate. A modern day Gilles Closson or Hippolyte Boulenger would have enjoyed painting the nearby Blue Ridge. If I had a business card, I would have given him one. Another gesture. Another connection. Another attempt to go the extra mile.

I just stuck out my hand and he shook it energetically.

"Merci," I said with my best accent. "Merci beaucoup."

7

The 9:49 to Paris-Nord

At the Liège-Guillemins train station, I ambled along one of the five white concrete platforms peeking in the windows of the 9:22 to Maastricht—a red train fading to pink that was only two passenger cars long. Each window presented a perfectly framed scene—an enigma, a once-upon-a-time, a universe. Woody Allen could have made a whole film based upon what any one of them suggested.

In one, two women sat facing each other, a liter of the universal symbol of pop friendship, Coca-Cola, commercially placed on the table between them. In another window, a man and a woman sat side by side, but were they together or just sitting together? Were they a couple or a pair? At the end of the train another man and woman sat opposite and knee-to-knee praying—or gazing solemnly at each other's crotch. I even spied my own curious self in the reflection of those plates of clean glass. What would Woody make of the story he saw in my face?

My family clustered around the schedule board at the center of the platform. I studied the time, the train numbers, and the platforms to make certain we were in the right place waiting for the right train. Rachel and John Mark perched on their suitcases and Benjamin and Joseph paced about them in a semicircle talking excitedly, wigwagging their hands. The 9:49 to Paris-Nord was on its way.

In WWII prostitutes worked the old train station, and Liège was a popular destination for soldiers at the front. Sex and desperation yielded consequences our troops may not have wanted to consider, but their officers had to. Venereal diseases could cripple our fighting machine. A soldier could face court-martial if he became disabled by VD. The army gave preventative shots before leave; if you still got VD and had a record of taking your shot, they'd let you slide.[23] There's a lot to keep straight in a war.

Dad never talked about such things as VD with me. Ever. The closest he came was telling me and three of my high school buddies that "a man's got needs." This was in the wake of discovering that one of our friends had knocked up his girlfriend. None of my friends' fathers talked with their sons about sex. We boys compared notes on this. My college roommate's dad came the closest. He told young Ronnie never to sleep with a girl if he wouldn't use her toothbrush. Back in college I thought this was crass but possibly useful information. All of this is to say that while Dad had leave in London, Boston, Indiana, and Fort Sill, he never had leave on the few days in Belgium he was at the front, hunkered as he was in the freezing woods, in fox holes, in snow and slush and the quiet prelude of the roar and smoke and confusion of battle.

As Rachel and our kids yucked it up with each other, I ventured to guess that no one on that wide, clean train platform in Liège had VD on their minds. I took another long look at the schedule board to make sure we were standing on the correct platform. A train finally pulled in—apparently the right one—and we grabbed our bags and piled on. Once on board, I practically vibrated with excitement. I high-fived the boys, and settled next to Rachel to drink in the summery colors that began flowing past.

Arrival in the bowels of Paris-Nord just after lunch was a cruel awakening. Cavernous and crowded, the Paris-Nord rail station serves 190 million passengers a year. (New York's Grand Central Terminal serves just under 25 million.) The building itself is a beautiful rat's maze of gleaming floors and high, ornate ceilings. How do you get to the Métro? Is the Métro the same thing as the RER? Where do you get passes, tokens, tickets? Orderly arrivals of centipede-lines of elementary children suited up for field trips marched single-file through the crowds. Other, grim legions weren't as polite as they barged through, all elbows and grumbles. Everyone else seemed to know exactly where they were going. We did not. We knew only one thing: we were in the way of people who knew where they were going.

We stood in a ticket line. Lot's of people were in the line, and the woman behind the glass way, way up front surely could tell us what we needed to do. I relaxed. There was something comforting about standing in a long line. It's completely democratic. Your turn is coming and so is mine. When some fellow in a white robe some distance in front of us uttered the word *Istanbul*, however, I presumed the woman behind the counter didn't have a ticket to our hotel.

We studied the Métro map our travel agent had given us. We studied the Métro maps on the walls and at the myriad kiosks in the station. Like rising water in a clogged toilet, our collective nervousness was rising. I asked a guard in a glassed-in booth, "Do you speak English?" No, he said. I tried asking in my botched version of French. "Parlez-vous anglais?" No, again, this time with a bigger smile. He seemed glad not to know English, to be letting us down. I forced my smile to match his.

There were a million places to go, hundreds of trains to catch, dozens of escalators to ride, steep stairs to negotiate, levels to explore, shops, turnstiles, corridors all leading somewhere, but where? One combination of passages would lead us to our destination, but which? The brittle conversations intensified. Joseph and Rachel were at odds about how to get to the same point on the building map. He insisted we proceed to another floor, and down the ill-lit tunnel *over there*. She was adamant that we needed to stay on the floor we were on and try the turnstiles *by the big windows*. Both needed to be right.

And both inched rapidly to meltdown. Benjamin tried to stay out of it, but in order to maintain cred with his bro, ultimately sided with Joseph, which didn't suit Rachel in the least. John Mark insisted everyone remain calm. I wanted to thank him, and I wanted to strangle him.

What's the stereotype? Who knows best when the family is confounded and confused? Who has the answers? Who adjusts his stance so the shaft of light from above illumines his square jaw and strong shoulders at the best possible angle? After a long moment of held breath who utters Truth and Wisdom in a silky baritone? On a stretch of glassy floor in the bowels of Gare du Nord, amidst the pushing mobs of travelers, in a knot of five quarrelsome people . . . it was certainly not me. I didn't know where to go. I could make no sense of the maps, the signs, the arrows. There was nothing I could helpfully add to ease my family's increasingly desperate mood. The very best thing I could have done would have been to find an ice cream shop. But I, too, was muddled. Ice cream was too obvious.

When my family was lost growing up, Dad simply did as Mom directed. Getting lost was just another adventure that my father never seemed to mind. I am my father's son in so many ways, but not in this way. I buy the theory that the journey is the destination, but in practice I like knowing I'm on the right track.

A certain amount of discombobulation comes with travel. My dad's friend J.P. Dale moved from Hampton to Ohio after the war and took up banking. While my family could afford few trips in my growing up years, we drove the ten hours west to see the Dales in the 1970s. Mom rode shotgun in my dead grandfather's 1972 Chevy that we had inherited; Deda died right after he retired, and Baba didn't drive. We did not get lost.

On the way, in Wheeling, West Virginia, we visited a factory that sold hand-blown glass. I remember the flushing heat of the molten glass, the acrid smells of the workshop, the jars and vases on the shelves still taking shape as they cooled. Looking through the brittle glass created the illusion of being underwater in the Chesapeake Bay, swimming up and up towards the sheet of light at the surface, tiny bubbles racing your ascent through translucent, undulant greens.

In Dayton I was treated to another vision. I was nine and the Dales teenaged son thrust upon me his Playboy magazine collection. Like bubbles trapped in warm glass still taking shape, I could hardly make out what I was seeing. All those curves and nice ladies' faces. I had never imagined such things. Couldn't they afford pajamas? I didn't know what to make of their gymnastic poses in bed. They'd never fall asleep like that. And where were their penises?

His sister and their friends played *Truth or Dare* upstairs in the playroom. I hadn't lived long enough to play that game the way they were playing it. The boys queried the girls about female anatomy and the girls matter-of-factly answered, then the girls asked their version of the same questions. I was in way over my head.

I knew girls were different, of course. They usually had longer hair than boys, for one thing. They cried more easily than boys. They ran faster, but couldn't throw as well. Most of them smelled nice. I wasn't stupid. I knew girls were unusual creatures. But the girls in *Playboy* were cataclysmically different. And if I could believe my ears, so were the girls in Ohio.

By the time the topic of conception—or maybe contraception—came up, I couldn't follow the language they were speaking anymore, even though much of it sounded like English. They used words I had never, ever heard. The gears of my brain were spinning so rapidly they began to melt and to slip out of sync. I sunk well beneath the waves to a quiet, green place. I had already drowned but could still see. I floated heavily beneath turquoise waves pulsing slowly with light. I could not make out the muffled sounds from the strange world that was rising around me.

I sat quietly in the back seat of that tan Chevy Impala on the way home from our family trip to Dayton. My parents and I had been to very different places.

Like melting glass, I moved in slow motion at the train station in Paris. I took stock. I found some comfort knowing that we weren't on a sinking ship. The Gare du Nord is not the Titanic in the least. If need be, we could sleep here. There were certainly enough restaurants to stay fed. I reminded myself that we were safe here. Though we all wanted to get on with things, we were in no rush. We had credit cards and euros. We were a phone call away from the U.S. Embassy, the Green Berets, AAA. Someone would bail us out if things got too crazy. Someone here surely spoke English. And someone would help us. Eventually.

This mental exercise of taking stock, akin to the Lamaze breathing I learned with Rachel when we were preparing for the birth of our children, helped. I was able to look around again, as if for the first time, and see how large and bright this place was. And most of the people here seemed happy.

Paris-Nord was certainly not so difficult to figure out, I told myself. We had merely gotten gummed up in a puddle of bad karma. And like any father usually short of Truth and Wisdom, I had a viable, albeit expensive, plan B. I would step out of the station to the queue of taxis, and without a word show the driver our hotel name and address, which I had written on a piece of paper folded neatly in my back pocket. When we arrived at our apartment on the opposite side of Paris, I would calmly pay him the $4,000 fare. I'd let him pile our bags onto the sidewalk, give him a tip, and say with a flourish to my frazzled kin: "Our home away from home." I seriously hoped it would not come to that, but knowing I had options was a relief.

I found another woman in another glass cage. And because there was no line, I approached and led with my best accent, "Parlez-vous Français?"

"I speak French," she said in perfect English, "and I also speak English."

I could have kissed her. I tried to explain where we wanted to go without my bottom lip quivering. She leaned forward and, not condescendingly, spoke to me like I was a young Christopher Columbus who had become separated from his elementary school class field trip. She told me that we needed to catch the Métro. We needed the blue line to Charles de Gaulle Étoile. Yes, we'd have to use an automated kiosk to buy tickets. No, the RER wouldn't get us where we needed to go. She pointed in the direction of the appropriate hallway. She reminded me I needed to be on the bottom floor. A building map was just over there, she said, pointing again. "You're welcome," she said to my litany of *mercis*. She wanted me to have a nice day. She felt like an old friend. People help each other in emergencies. We all want to help each other through. Blessedly, she had helped me. I could have kissed her again.

What is it about my wanting to kiss train agents? I remembered wanting to lay one on the agent at the station in Brussels days before, and now wanting to kiss his slender, French counterpart. The man in Brussels was ruddy faced and not much to look at, but kind and helpful. This French agent was younger and infinitely more attractive in every way—rosy cheeks, thick, brown hair pulled into a tidy pony tail, green eyes, freckles scampering across the bridge of a milky white nose. The urge to kiss both agents was comparatively the same, regardless of appearances. Was I simply attracted to all representatives of European rail services, or did the desire to kiss them have something more to do with standard protocol when confronted by angels of mercy? Maybe I just didn't know what to do with my thankful lips.

Even though it still took a while to find the right hallway, we found it. Finally. We force fed the ticket kiosk with Euros because it insisted on spitting out our credit card. We and our luggage bumped through the temperamental turnstiles. We emerged from subterranean shadows to a distant, outdoor platform. When the first Métro train rattled noisily into the station, we shouldered into the last car, folding ourselves tightly into the packed throng onboard, and, for better or worse, left that purgatory of endless hallways for the heavenly streets of Paris.

John Mark ventured some small talk. "I wonder what humans would be like without shoulders?" His bright face wilted when he realized I had no insight on the subject. I smiled anyway and he smiled weakly back as the train jerked around an impossibly tight curve.

Believing that what doesn't kill you makes you stronger, I knew Paris had better, richer, bigger surprises in store.

Despite the fact that the train lurched and creaked unsteadily, our collective mood seemed to be lifting. A sign on the sliding door against which I was trying not to lean warned against trapping our hands. *Finger weg von den Turen,* the caption began in German. The man playing accordion at the front of the car wore an expression indicating nothing short of eschatological satisfaction, which communicated that everything was going to be fine—in this life and in the next. At our end of the crowded car there was a disproportionate number of elbows. I reluctantly inhaled a host of interesting body odors, ours included. Antsy kids were practically shouting. I tried to stay clear of that door plastered with warnings. *No pongas las manos.* The train jolted in such an old man, palsied way that I thought we might tip off the tracks. We picked up speed and hit the curves like drunken, Olympic bobsledders. But we were moving, possibly in the right direction. And I believed that together we would still find our way.

We found the apartment, got lost for an hour on our walk home from the grocery ten-minutes away, and eventually settled in for the night. Rachel and I cooked a big spaghetti dinner in the tiniest kitchen I had ever stood next to. A modest sink fit into the recessed wall. The four burner electric stove could not hold two Spaghetti pots at once. The oven could possibly handle a large chicken, but a pigeon or a few quail would be a better fit, or, maybe, a smallish *magret de canard.* A Thanksgiving turkey would require quartering, at least, before a very tight insertion, but who celebrated Thanksgiving in Paris? Beneath the counter was a Barbie-homemaker-sized dishwasher and fridge pre-stocked with a half-dozen mini-bottles of brown liquor.

What this kitchenette lacked in horizontal space, it made up vertically. Above the stamp-sized counters were four cabinets that stretched to the ceiling; Rachel would require a trampoline to reach the top shelf. Beneath the ample cabinets hung a microwave. In order to *work in the kitchen,* you had to stand in the hallway. The aisle on the Eurostar was the size of a small continent by way of comparison.

The thought suddenly hit me as I stood in this Lilliputian kitchen that small as it is, it is more than adequate, and our journey compared to Dad's is luxury. He never had such nice digs in all of Europe. As Dad got closer to the front, GIs ate mostly from the backs of kitchen trucks under the cover of tarps, more often than not under open air. Their lives were crammed in haversacks stuffed with personal belongings, letters from home, souvenirs. Their mess kit consisted of a fork, knife, and spoon made of tin plated or rust resistant steel. They may have had a Garand bayonet in among the postcards from home and their entrenching tool and medical kit, which included a one-size fits all bandage impregnated with sulfa. They carried a canteen and a small grocery store of combat food rations: three "K" rations, three "D" rations (1,800 calories per dark chocolate bar made by Hershey's able to withstand 120-degrees Fahrenheit), four ration-heating units and water purification tablets. Judging from the number of war journals kept by GIs, some carried a leaky ballpoint pen or pencil and a notebook. They always were loaded with raincoat, blanket, shelter half, and shaving kit. Dad's M1941 or M1943 field jacket and wool pants were treated with CC-2 anti-gas paste. The war crated gigantic machines for death and stripped the individual of most personal effects.

Our small, top floor apartment was completely sufficient. Everyone but Rachel—who rises five feet and two inches above the soles of her tennis shoes—had to watch his head for the slanted, low ceilings. The windows cranked out, and you could lean out and see the enclosed courtyard six-stories below. Red flowers and ivy crept up the otherwise dingy looking walls from flowerboxes on the first floor. Windows of the lower apartments were closed and curtained. You could see across other rooftops and look into upper story windows, which, like ours, were opened to slants of sun. White towels and underclothes fluttered like surrender flags over the wrought iron window rails of other apartments.

Our two bedrooms allowed for modest elbowroom. Benjamin and Joseph shared a room with two ironing-board-sized beds. They split a four-drawer dresser. They both could stand up, but only one at a time. The room was a perfect size for playing cards and having late night talks. Rachel and I got a queen bed, a TV, a dresser, and a wall-sized mirror that captured our every move. John Mark had more space but less privacy. He would sleep on the couch in the living room, which doubled as the dining room and hallway to the bathroom.

The antique bathtub had unusually high sides, but lacked sufficient length for stretching out; after you had soaped up and sipped a few glasses of Beaujolais, you could drown if you simply pulled up your knees. The shower was sufficient, but I had to kneel to wet anything above my collarbone. And much to the kids' great pleasure, our bathroom came equipped with a bidet, which they had never before seen the likes of. In a city replete with treasures like the Louvre and the Royal Palace, it was good to know that it took no more than a porcelain appliance to impress our children. After we explained what it was, turn by turn, each son emerged from exploratory tonic colonics wearing otherworldly expressions. A roller coaster couldn't have thrilled them more.

We liked our digs. The spotless rooms were refreshingly decorated with newly painted, mint colored walls. We each had a soft bed on which to sleep. We had a trendy glass dining room table with five chairs that swiveled. We had each other. And most of all, we had a bidet.

On this first Parisian evening, prime rib and sautéed scallops couldn't have tasted better—though it might have been impossible to coax a meal like that from such a small, underpowered kitchen. I felt as if we'd come all the way from another planet to get here and now I yearned for a shower and bed. As we prayed over steaming spaghetti, I thought of Dad. He was alive in my head. I could feel his eagerness in my body. "Gosh," I could almost hear him say. "From all the way across the ocean, and now here we are. *Grand Paree!*" I'm certain that Jesus had something like this in mind when he shared communion with his disciples. They would always be connected. They would always remember. That feast would never fail to fill and to delight. Together we are the communion of saints: Sebastian pierced with arrows, my sleepy looking wife across the glass table, my laughing boys eating the last of three buttered baguettes, both the unhelpful train clerks and the angelically helpful ones, strangers of every sort, and even my dear, dead father. All present and accounted for.

There should be a point after dinner when you just sit back and let things sink in. I was full to the point of loosening my belt. We may have felt a lot of things at that moment, but all of us probably felt something akin to satisfaction. It was a very good feeling. John Mark broke the silence.

"Penguins," he said.

Rachel said, "Huh?" Joseph glowered—a look that took him all of his teenage years to hone, refashion, rehearse, and then to master. Benjamin added, "What, what?" Where was the youngest one among us coming from? Had a spring come loose in his largish, twelve-year-old head? I sliced another wedge of camembert.

"If humans didn't have shoulders," John Mark announced with a cherubic smile, "we'd all look like penguins."

8

Luminous Paris

On Sunday we walked to the American Church in Paris. Everywhere in Paris is a view, and every overlook along the Seine is entrancing. Generous morning light painted buildings and gardens in warm yellows, tans, and blues, and the river flashed deep greens and silver. Ernie Pyle, the prolific roving journalist who covered WWII for Scripps Howard Newspapers, arrived in Paris as she was being liberated from the Germans in August, 1944. "The streets were lined as they are by Fourth of July parade crowds at home, only this crowd was almost hysterical . . . [W]e were swarmed over and hugged and kissed and torn at. Everybody, even beautiful girls, insisted on kissing you on both cheeks." Writing about the liberation was difficult for Pyle. "Actually the thing floored most of us [war correspondents]. I felt totally incapable of reporting it . . . A good many of us feel we have failed to present adequately what was the loveliest, brightest story of our time. It may be that this was because we have been so unused, for so long, to anything bright."[24]

Dad's experience of Paris may have been very much the same. Arriving here days after his liberation in April 1945, the

City of Light pulsated. The bustle of the city, the architecture, the excitement of relieved people was a lovely, bright moment after such a long darkness. He was strong enough to sit in a jeep; but malnourished, he was too weak to hike along the Seine as we had. And Dad probably felt something that Pyle took for granted, which sweetened every breath and brightened every view. Freedom.

Our delicious, mile-long stroll took us out of the shadowed canyons of our neighborhood onto the wide, sunny sidewalks of New York Avenue. We crossed the Seine at the de l'Alma bridge, posing for pictures at the golden Liberty Torch, which melted in perfect sun. We didn't know this was the unofficial spot memorializing the death of Princess Diana who, along with Dodi Fayed and their driver, died in a crash in the nearby tunnel. Nor did we know—but we should have been able to guess—that the bridge was named to commemorate a battle, in this case of the Crimean War.

The church sanctuary was decked out for Pentecost with three, striking twenty-foot-long red cloths hanging down the organ pipes feathering to a point behind a simple wooden cross on the chancel. As dramatic as the banners were, the sanctuary didn't need additional decoration. Stained glass windows (two of which are Tiffany—the only two such windows in France), ornate stone arches and chandeliers, and a vaulted ceiling were decoration enough. The soaring ceiling does what it was designed to do—draws worshippers' eyes up beyond the fetters of mortar and bricks towards the divine. I felt like royalty sitting unrushed with my family on the padded pew. I couldn't read every emotion on their faces, but *expectation* was impossible to miss. I think I saw belonging, too, something akin to contentment. For my family, church is home.

The music was a wormhole into another dimension. The organist wove together hymn tunes for the first part of the prelude; a strong baritone sang Handel for the second part. The congregational singing was rousing. The full congregation—about 600 souls—didn't hold back.

We passed the peace with those in the pews near us. I found the diversity of race, dress, and ages thrilling. Faces of every color and English speakers from some fifty nations and 35 Christian denominations call the American Church in Paris their home. Worshipping with them in such a magnificent space was electric.

Except for a brief season in junior high school when I thought I might drop dead from boredom, I've always loved the church. Always the first to be ready on Sundays, Dad put on what he called his Sunday-go-to-hell clothes, and Mom doused herself from the giant bottle of pungent-smelling perfume I was tricked into buying her every Mothers' Day. We piled into the car for the fifteen-minute drive to Community Presbyterian Church. The Sunday roads through my hometown were nearly empty and nobody hurried. Dad coasted slowly over the Pembroke Avenue bridge so that we could get an unrushed look at Hampton Creek, its green marshes dotted with white heron.

Mom picked out his ties and Dad wore them short. They were wide and stopped at his belly button, not his belt. I thought he looked comical, like a TV show gangster. The patterns and colors she chose—maroons, greys, unflattering shades of yellow—could make you dizzy. Have brown, silver, and forest green in one outfit much less a single necktie ever been a trending fashion? When he died years later and Mom asked if I wanted any of his ties I almost asked, *"Are you kidding?"* Of course I should have kept a few. I would like to run my hand through my fifty or so ties knowing that some were his, though there's not a remote chance I'd ever put one on.

The pastor preached intelligibly with warmth; half of the people in these pews may have been tourists whom he would never see again, but the other half were his flock, and I knew what it's like looking out into faces of those charged to your care. After the sermon, we read aloud a Pentecost litany featuring fourteen languages at once. Unrushed silences breathed life into the words we spoke as stained glass windows bent ordinary light into a strange, wondrous alchemy. Rainbow colored light saturated the room.

I feasted on the singing. These were not tired hymns accompanied by a warbling, funeral parlor electronic organ.

This organist set the 116-pipe Beckerath on fire, giving both it and the congregation a strenuous work out. Nothing dragged. The king of instruments grabbed our words and slung them against the walls and ceiling. Nor did the congregation drone when they sang; congregants let it rip, singing with energy and volume.

I remember singing with Dad. He took me to the Men's Conference at Massanetta Springs' church camp in Virginia's Shenandoah Valley when I was a teen. Each lecture and service of worship in the open-air pavilion began with singing. I cringed to hear Dad sing loudly. While he loved singing, no matter the tune, he sung unerringly to a combination of Dixie and Amazing Grace. And he sounded like a car horn.

I was a teenager and fitting in meant everything. But at the men's conference, Dad *did* fit in. Every man sang about as badly—and loudly. The swelling song of four hundred men was mighty, not unlike the Friday night din of a Hampton Crabbers football contest. Making a joyful noise as the psalmist implores seemed their goal, which they achieved brilliantly with equal parts joy and, well, reckless *noise*. Watching my dad have so much fun made me have fun, too. Ever since, that's how I've approached congregational singing. What they did wasn't art. But it was worship, and it was exciting to be caught up in.

Six days into our European journey, I was content in this gothic space, so glad to be sitting on padded pews, free from having to make decisions about directions from hard-to-follow maps. I let my mind wander through this familiar, reformed liturgy without fear of getting lost—which may be the best definition of *sanctuary* there is.

After worship the associate pastor chatted with us as if this were a small, rural parish and we were the only guests she'd seen in months. She brightened when we told her about my dad. The church, she said, was a gathering place for GIs during and after the war. A dorm downstairs housed men on leave. There were dances in the gym. Church members took soldiers around the city for cultural tours.

Feeling sentimental, I led my family to the basement and asked Rachel to take my picture in the gym. Dad would have been too frail after the war to play basketball on that wooden floor. I could picture him wearing number 23 on the George Wythe Junior High basketball team. But he might have slow-danced once or twice in this very gym. At just over a hundred pounds after his release, he could muster neither the stamina nor balance to dance a whole song. He certainly would have liked hearing music for a change instead of cannon blasts and moaning, sick men. These thoughts knocked the wind out of me.

At an open-air market a few blocks behind the church, we lounged on the warm, sunny patio and ordered rotisserie chicken from the café. Benjamin and Joseph devoured one chicken each. Benjamin, his lips glistening from a juicy leg, declared, "this is the best chicken I've ever eaten." Not having to rush made me realize how pressed we had been during the trip to make our next destination. We all had gotten weary of ham and butter sandwiches on the go. Here we sat outdoors in bright sun and smiled and laughed and, for the first time on our trip, took our time.

Artists sold jewelry on felt-covered folding tables set up on the wide sidewalks. Flower vendors wrapped ungainly gladiolas in sheets of colored paper for men in Sunday suits; to whom were these men taking such boss flowers? Couples strolled, ancient women walked their groomed poodles and panting mutts, children bounced and darted around their parents' legs playing tag.

As shops began closing for the afternoon, we reluctantly eased out of our chairs sniffing out a smidgeon of dessert. Gelato from a pushcart vendor satisfied our desire for both zesty flavor and eye-popping color; I got something orange. Rachel's scoop was purple. These were Clemson University colors, and Joseph was bound for garnet and black at the University of South Carolina. He didn't notice this accidental treason, but I did; I thought for a moment how his life was getting ready to launch from the sure fires of home into a dorm and classrooms only 90-minutes but light years away from me. I went to college, too. I remember how on the first visit home I wasn't the same person I was when I left. I watched him devouring his gelato, a culinary acrobat—

walking, pontificating over his brothers, leading them, laughing, expertly wielding his tongue to catch every melting drop from his cone. This taste explosion was a remarkable end to our meal, the cones lasting only a few blocks. We wound through the Sixth Arrondissement, dodging Sunday traffic— mainly brainy looking young professionals with dogs on long leashes—across Saint-Germain towards the Seine and Notre Dame, our next stop. Locking onto our destination, we picked up our pace and began making time with the Seine sliding away on our left and a deadline in mind.

It took 170 years to build Notre Dame and it could take that long to tour it adequately. John Mark noted the edifice didn't resemble what he had expected from Disney's *Hunchback*. We dutifully posed for pictures, nevertheless, and deftly elbowed our way through crowds towards the massive doors.

Before my eyes adjusted to the dim and as I looked up to that impossibly high ceiling, I bumped into a steel rail groin-high at the Chapel of Maccabees. I doubled over. The life-like statuary coolly stared me down, unsympathetic to my pain. Craftsmen had transformed every nook, arch, and wall into a masterpiece. It was stunning: the iron and stone work, gold crosses covered in filigree, fluted columns rising like sturdy trees, and elegant carvings. All of this beauty was gilded with a greater beauty—light filtering through stained glass. When the educator Emma Willard first saw the interior of the cathedral at Rouen on her passage from Le Havre to Paris, she wrote in her journal, "[M]y mind was smitten with a feeling of sublimity almost too intense for mortality."[25] I understood. At Notre Dame, the best I could do was to sit down in one of the simple wooden chairs filling the nave and be quiet.

Keeping my mouth shut was easy. My family had scattered. There was nobody for me to talk with except God. I wasn't sure, however, I could calm my incessant interior chatter. Voices careened around in my brain: We faced a lengthy walk back to the apartment. I imagined the many steps. I should allow time for perusing the gift shop. Since John Mark planted the seed, Esmeralda in Disney's *Hunchback* was a fox. What's the upkeep on a place like this? I wondered how my discreet snapshots would turn out in such dusky light. There's no way to describe this place. *Dad was here.*

My father was right here.

Did Dad—like me—require a few long moments to settle the clatter in his head? He had more things in it to calm. The war had been so noisy. He never once talked to me about his prayer life, even whether or not he had one. He led what he might have thought was the obligatory dinner prayer. He bowed in worship, perhaps to give his eyes a rest, perhaps because he endeavored to fit in, perhaps to better see the one to whom he was talking. His prayers were definitely private and silent; were they also conversational, like his son's, and sometimes constant? We never talked about prayer when I was growing up, and beyond our shared church pew and dinner table at home, we never practiced it, either. Did he pray at Notre Dame in the late spring of 1945?

The nave is so confoundingly large, I wondered if Dad's aged prayers could still be bouncing off the stone, glass, and wood. I wondered if another creature, with finer senses, could somehow dial them in. When the tourists go home, do the seraphim shake off their marble and fly around? Do they grab old prayers and wrestle them into song? I tried but could not snatch any of Dad's words that might have floated like dust motes in bands of colored light. If I heard anything from the past in that space it was the tears and the awe, and my sense of hearing has been so dulled by years of television commercials. I realized it is likely Dad sat a long, long time in an uncomfortable chair like the one I occupied and never uttered a word. Silence is prayer, too.

Far from home, did he find comfort? I feel at home in quiet church sanctuaries. Did he? Notre Dame is a far cry from the Hampton Baptist Church of his childhood, but the hush was similar. And the muted light. And the care given the furnishings. He may have found a moment of peace here. I felt that peace. I hoped he did. God knows he needed it.

I sat. I listened. Any chattering the hushed crowds made vanished into the air perfumed with candle-smoke below that 108-foot ceiling. I listened and watched the faithful kneel, genuflect, crane their necks at the stunning craftsmanship in every direction. A few pests snapped pictures and I resisted the urge to slap them. Mostly, though, visitors were doing what I was doing. They were being astounded.

I wondered how Dad might have taken the muffled quiet of the Cathedral of Notre Dame in late April of 1945. The war had been so loud, the suffering so close.

Within a year of returning home, Dad enrolled at the College of William and Mary on the GI Bill. He didn't last. "couldn't take it," he said. He told me once how during a lecture in a quiet classroom, somebody's pencil rolled down a slant-top desk and bounced benignly on the hardwood floor. In the split-second before it clattered to a stop, he had dived under a desk for cover.

Dad's sister Alice remembers riding with their mother to pick him up in Williamsburg. She was 10-years-old at the time. He looked happy to see them, Alice said. He was relieved to leave the college from which his kid sister would later graduate with honors.

It's difficult sitting in a classroom after having squatted in a war zone. The war was filled with noise. And the silences of war are filled with other kinds of terror. Sebastian Junger writing about American troops in Afghanistan believes the quiet of waiting is the hardest part of war, next to the killing and the dying.

"A fellow has kind of a cumulative fright after he has had a really close one," wrote Ernie Pyle. "[A]ll of us will have to make our return to normal life gradually and in small doses."[26] Pyle never got the chance. The war ended for him when he was killed on le Shima, an island near Okinawa in April, 1945.

I found John Mark bobbing through the crowd. I joined him, and we explored the side chapels and windows. The long lines killed whatever interest we had to climb the famed towers. We wandered outside and found ourselves buying water at a café with a view of the side of the cathedral. Forty minutes later the family met us on the plaza out front beneath the dour faces of the kings of Israel. The stone gargoyles stood frozen in their mid-air leap from the towers. We hadn't done this place justice, but it was time to go.

Unless we caught the Métro, we had about a five-mile walk to get back to our apartment. Facing west, it felt like 500 miles. We set out along the Right Bank this time, but with every tired step, all I could think about was a nap. This was a crime, I knew. Paris deserved more from me than yawns. Rachel, however, was in her element. She believes walking, like gardening, is sacramental. I can outpace my bride, but I cannot out-walk her. She's hiked to the bottom of the Grand Canyon and back, run what is called a hash race through Indonesian jungle, and conquered sub-freezing headwinds in Evanston winters in order to get from a graduate dorm to a Starbucks. She showed no signs of winding down. But I was fading. I had given up trying to convince myself that there was nothing more glorious than a Sunday walk along the Seine.

We passed fishermen with bamboo poles casting lines into the river. A few couples lounged on blankets spread out on the grass, wicker baskets of food between them. The river took its time. Power walkers sped by us in a smooth rush. Older couples held hands. My boys cut up and laughed. They were making good time. I was barely keeping up. I tried to be happy for the romantic lovers, the contented fishermen, the trim speed walkers. This effort failed. I was simply ragged out. But my bride was in her zone, her face set like polished stone facing in the direction of our apartment.

When you don't want to do it, walking any distance is too far.

Even in Paris.

9

Normandy

I ask you
To witness—
The shovel is brother to the gun.
—Carl Sandburg, Iron, Chicago Poems

Monday we went to Normandy. Dense clouds and drizzle combined to make perfect conditions for sleeping late, especially after a day of traipsing over Paris, but our departure from the bus station required being ready for a taxi at 6:15. Waiting in the hotel lobby, we looked like zombies.

The snappy taxi driver appeared at the front desk and frowned when he counted his fare. Two families had gathered for the ride to the tour bus, but both wouldn't fit into his cab. His taxi, only slightly larger than an American grocery cart, could seat five mashed into the seats. With this other family, polite but not interested in talking with us, we totalled eight. When our sons were little, we could have squeezed them onto our laps in a pinch. To do so now would have required rolling down the windows and sawing off the roof.

Deflated, the portly driver apologized, yanked a cell phone out of his tight front pocket, and started yelling. I presumed he was ordering another driver with a van—which is what the hotel clerk had arranged for us the night before. I wondered if we'd make it to the bus on time, but before I could get worked up, a new driver bustled into the lobby and drove us in the morning dark to the tour company.

It was raining and warm. Shops near the tour company were closed. Our bus was ready, but it was not time to board. We paced around the covered sidewalks peering in the windows of La Cure Gourmande. This was cruel. The biscuits, confiseries, and chocolats oozed delectability; canisters of hot chocolate and red and gold foil boxes of sweets were stacked in tantalizing displays only a few inches from our sniffing noses. But we could not smell them, we could not touch, and we could not taste.

Once on the bus, the boys settled into the reclining seats, inserted their ear pods, and zoned out. The bus groaned past weeping storefronts on the empty Rue de Rivoli, taking wide turns onto other deserted streets. The Obelisque stood guard over Tulieries Garden. It was Pentecost holiday. It seemed Paris would never wake up, locked forever beneath a greasy dome of glass. I watched the rain streak diagonally down the windows until I jostled away to sleep.

Dad didn't splash to shore on a Normandy beach in June, 1944. He walked, 5 months later, high and dry on a gangplank into Le Havre, fifty or so miles north of the nearest D-Day beaches. Rachel and I both wanted our kids to see the landing beaches at Normandy, even if Dad didn't, because we wanted them to see how costly it was for the Allies to reclaim the continent. Nowhere, perhaps, is that message more somberly communicated than at the Normandy American Cemetery at Colleville-sur-Mer. We wanted our sons to stand before the last resting places, rank upon rank of them, marked by precisely arranged gravestones. The men who died on the beaches and cliffs opened the way for the men who would die in the nearby hedgerows who, in turn, made it possible to fight in the Belgian forest and beyond the Rhine, until the killing stopped and the war in Europe, finally, ended.

It was at this cemetery and the beaches to the south that Steven Spielberg set the opening and closing scenes of his movie *Saving Private Ryan*. Dad and I saw the film when it came out in 1998. Droves of veteran's groups watched it together. They talked to reporters about how those fifty-year-old memories were still vivid.

As we drove to this movie, I was afraid it might set off live ordinance, long buried. I feared that this movie might bring it all back for my father. I vaguely worried that Dad might have a heart attack, or come apart in some sort of post traumatic stress explosion of regret and sorrow, and that the family would blame me for his demise. I asked him to go with me because it seemed this was the sort of excursion fathers and sons ought to take. So, we went. I tried to be calm.

The theater was full with an inordinate number of old men in cardigans with canes and doting elderly couples. This wasn't a chick flick or teen magnet. I noticed more that one pair of what I imagined were fathers with their grown sons as cinema wingmen, chauffeurs, witnesses. Anthony Lane wrote in his *New Yorker* review of the film that this "is as credible and confounding vision of Hell as could be imagined." He was speaking of the rushing, 27-minute, almost bottomless drop that starts the movie. The gates of landing craft crash open, the beaches appear, and soldiers immediately start getting killed. When the closing credits rolled, I dreaded the house lights, even more the sun.

Walking out of the theater, I remember trying to clear a path for my shuffling Dad, of whom I was mightily proud in a confused way. The able bodied in the crowd gave wide berth to those who hobbled, to the vets donning ball caps emblazoned with USN or military pins. My dad could have *been* the elderly Private Ryan at the end of the movie, trembling at the bone white crosses and six-pointed stars in the Normandy American Cemetery, asking out loud for affirmation, pleading with his withered wife to tell him that his life had been worth saving in the first place.

As we made our way down the carpeted hallway to the parking lot, I couldn't bear to look into anyone's eyes, my dad's especially. We all took one another in through our fine-tuned, peripheral vision. We all saw one another, heads down, shuffling out quietly. Even though many others had red eyes, I still felt embarrassed for having such a wet face; it was just a movie. I still sniffled back sobs. Dad was stoic.

I wanted to talk to Dad, but couldn't. When I tried, I could feel something big and hollow inside of me about to become unmoored. So, I held onto my words. I studied my blue t-shirt just to make sure it wasn't too wet from all my ridiculous crying. The tears didn't show, but a bunch of little white crescent shaped things did. They were sprinkled down my chest like giant flakes of dandruff. At first I thought it was popcorn, but I hadn't eaten any. Then I identified them: they were bits and pieces of fingernails which I vaguely remembered having chewed. My fingers couldn't have tolerated a double feature.

In the car on the way home I risked speaking. "What did you think?" I asked. "Was it like that? Was it realistic?"

After a moment he said, "It was just like that." Then the zinger: "Except it was worse." I tried to pay attention to the traffic lights. Coliseum Drive was an obstacle course. "All the killing nowadays," he said, voice trailing off. "I don't understand it. They kill and they don't even know why they do it. These drive by shootings. Gangs. It doesn't make sense." I'm certain he'd be unable to comprehend modern day terrorism, kidnappings, and televised beheadings.

For a man who doesn't say much, it had been a talkative day.

By nine o'clock, after nearly 150 miles of speeding through morning rain on France's oldest motorway, the A13, we spilled out of the sleek bus onto a blacktop parking lot near the coast. Testing my legs, I could smell salt in the muggy air. Our two young guides pointed to a long concrete sidewalk towards the Mémorial de Caen. Black thunderheads rafted across the sky revealing patches of clear blue. This sky flicked a few large drops of stinging rain.

Inside, a Spitfire hung from the high ceiling in a lobby. The lobby connected to a labyrinthine catacomb of dim hallways. The bright, open space narrowed as we moved deeper into exhibits that explained not only the story of the largest invasion in modern times but the war's political and psychosocial antecedents. Rachel tried to keep up with the boys who scurried through the halls like curious rats sniffing through a maze for a prize. I vaguely remembered being their age when everything was a race. In no rush, I immediately became engrossed in the pictures and displays.

One exhibit pictured hundreds of Hitler Youth—2.3 million strong in 1933—standing at attention in straight lines, each head of hair combed and meticulously parted, saluting Hitler. He had just been elected chancellor. Thirty-percent of the German workforce was unemployed. In Virginia, Dad was playing war and baseball with neighborhood 9-year-olds; he and his friends would have been unable to find Germany on the map.

As I stood in Caen peering at the photo and those neat rows of *Hitlerjugend,* all I could think about was how these teens in short pants wore such warm looking socks. Dad needed thick, dry socks like that when he was a POW. Instead, his feet were always cold and often wet in the winter of 1945. He almost lost them.

With third and fourth degree frostbite, not only does the surface skin freeze, but also the deeper muscles, tendons, blood vessels, and nerves. The skin becomes hard and waxy. Untreated extreme frostbite may result in fingers and toes simply falling off. Frostbite has to do with being cold. By contrast, trench foot has to do with being wet. Advanced trench foot often involves blisters and open sores leading to fungal infections, which may begin as a harmless-seeming white or yellow spot under the tip of a toenail. As the nail fungus spreads deeper into the nail, the nail yellows, thickens, and develops crumbling edges.

Twenty-five years after the war, without his ever making a point of it, whenever I'd see Dad's feet I'd imagine the harrowing, wintery-wet steps he trudged in 1944 and 1945. His nails were thick and yellow, like the crust of some cheeses.

They didn't hurt him when I was a kid, but seeing them made something in me hurt. At Caen I stood before that picture looking at row upon row of Nazi youth in warm, dry knee socks; I wanted to strangle somebody.

Halos of soft light ring each museum display. When patrons bowed into the light, they took on the countenance of curious angels; when they stepped back, they were swallowed by the anonymity of the dark. The wide halls allowed plenty of room even for these several busloads of patrons. The dark concealed the tears.

One display reported "Out of the 4,918 Jewish children deported from Belgium to Auschwitz, 53 would come back." As many as 5,800,000 Jews were murdered in the Holocaust; 1,250,000 of that number were children. One in ten survived. When the war ended in Europe, no more than 120,000 Jewish children were still alive, mainly in Western Europe. "In whole regions of Central and Eastern Europe, not a single Jewish child still lived."

Understandably, while the museum is spacious, things began to feel close. After an hour, it was doing me in: the pictures of saluting youth, the informative display captions surgically placed on every wall, the video footage and newsreels of events such as Kristallnacht and the carnage of the D-Day invasion. After 90 minutes, I was wearing paper thin, reaching such mental and emotional overload that I began to wonder if I had the energy to absorb the actual landing beaches that we had come to see. I remembered what Bill Bryson wrote about the Belgian villages and countryside flattened by the war. "It was impossible to imagine that this perpetually tranquil place had been the epicenter, more or less, of the Battle of the Bulge . . . I simply couldn't take it in—that these terrible, savage things had happened here, in these hills and woods, to people as close to me in time as my father."[27] The Caen Memorial was crushing and beautiful and too much for just one visit.

I fought the temptation to be cynical. Hitler's genocide, after all, wasn't the last. The cycles of violence around the world keep spinning.

Dad wasn't an idealist, but he wasn't a cynic, either. When his cousin Penny Donne from California visited Virginia, Dad took her and her husband to the Air and Space Museum in downtown Hampton, where a restored 1920 merry-go-round spun delighted children in dizzy circles.

Dad wanted people to have a good time. Do no harm. Live and let live. If you can't say anything nice, don't say anything at all. It's okay just to laugh, to horse around, to enjoy an ear of summer corn. When Dad smiled, which he did often, people smiled back.

On a hot August afternoon next to the museum, the lights of the restored 1920 carousel are flashing and the calliope music calls. Smiling horses glide up and down and circle smoothly like planets in dependable orbit. Children can't decide which painted horse to pick. Grandparents take pictures.

Come on, Dad said to Penny and Frank. *Who says just the kids get to have all the fun?*

"How many people take their adult cousins on a merry-go-round?" Penny asked me some years ago. "I think your dad was the most 'up' person I have ever known."

They rode until they got dizzy. And why not? God knows there's enough pain in the world. Despite the pain—or maybe because of it—Dad gave his inner child space in which to play. He became a grown man committed to Sunday drives, giant bowls of ice cream, and TV movies. He never failed watching the sunset. He paid close attention to bird song. And if he was ever near a merry-go-round, he paid his money, and took a ride.

This memory was a happy moment in the dark halls of Caen.

I sat silently on the short bus ride to the beaches. The clouds and threat of rain were gone for now. The bus nosed into the parking lot at La Pointe du Hoc beneath shafts of sun.

Grass grows right up to the rocky cliffs overlooking the Atlantic. Three hundred Rangers shot ropes up the cliff and attacked like knights climbing castle walls. By the end of D-Day only ninety were able enough to return to battle. The day we were there, gulls cartwheeled in the wind. On the beach far below, a speck of a man was working two surf-fishing poles. If the land were for sale, it would fetch a fortune because who wouldn't be enthralled with the lavish view?

Except the land isn't for sale. No picnics allowed. This is a place of remembrance, not a disc golf park. At the end of the point stands a steel reinforced concrete battery where Germans trained guns up and down the beaches on both sides of that stony outcropping of rocks. The manicured lawn is pocked by allied bomb craters. The craters have weathered. They've softened over time. Standing at the edge of them, children screeched for their parents' attention; when the parents turned to look, they launched down the slopes, squealing with delight to the bottom of the bowl. Only gulls, distant waves, and laughing children broke the quiet.

A month before our trip, the Riverside High School Band featured James Barnes' "Lonely Beach" as part of its spring concert. Had band director Mr. Vrieze not introduced it, only the most historically tuned-in would connect this song to any of the lonely beaches along the Normandy coast on June 6, 1944.

The kids called him Vrieze, and as he seized the podium, a dozen teens from the drum line skipped off the stage taking places at various percussion instruments planted all around the auditorium. These had gone unnoticed until this dramatic moment: a kettle drum at the entrance doors in the back, a snare on the floor near the stage, a wind machine halfway up the center aisle, chimes by the wall near the exit sign.

The song began serenely, no small feat for eighty teens largely new to their rented instruments. A silver screen went down in my brain. I saw gulls, waves, and heard gentle breezes in the rise and fall of song. Like a gathering wind, the song swelled in volume and intensity and became a commanding *force* in the auditorium. By now, all of these kids were playing their hearts out, music building louder and louder. They deftly turned the pages of their music with a snap, their faces glowing red, sitting up straight, hovering over their swimming notes, playing as loudly as they could. A dissonance, like a twister taunting a field of corn, began rising from the sound, its tail touching down flirtatiously like a record player needle in a shaking hand being set down on a slightly warped stereophonic LP. This dissonance was not a few accidental wrong notes, a common enough feature in high school concerts. This was a movement taking form and building speed—like a locomotive.

That was when I noticed the jarring bangs, clangs, and rattles of unexpected, not entirely musical sounds from beyond the stage, from the aisles and the back near the doors and on the floor stage right and left. I turned and saw these kids jerking to the beat, pounding their instruments, rocking and lost in another world. And they weren't the only ones. There was Vrieze on whom everyone drew a bead. He stood on the podium slashing the air with both arms, rising to his toes, keeping the solid beat. He was glaring at them with directorial, hawk eyes one moment, then squeezing his eyes shut the next, nodding to the music wrought from the barely calloused hands of these teens.

The way these noises wove into the intensifying music from the stage cued up the landing. I saw bombs pulverizing fields, smoking metal streaming from hot guns, landing craft slamming upon the beach, shrieks of men being torn to shreds on the sand, being killed at water's edge, killing, cursing, dying.

My heart pounding, I watched these lovely kids on stage; Joseph with his clarinet was among them. I looked over at Mom sitting next to me, the laugh lines of her face hardened to a somber mask. I imagined her as a pretty 16-year-old watching newsreels of the war at Saturday matinees at the Paramount on the corner of Washington Avenue and 29th in downtown Newport News. Her cousin Kinky was reported MIA for some months late in the war. She knew the horrors to which this music alluded. John Mark and Benjamin sat next to Rachel. What did they see? The stinging sand, the bullets burning into the men trying too late to pull their helmets down over their shoulders? Probably not. It was just another school concert to them. It was a tsunami for me.

As the song returned to the steady rhythm of gentle waves, as the storm of steel melted and the breeze cleared the smoke, I was covered in goose flesh. I couldn't possibly have been the only one weeping. In the long, hushed moment between practiced silence and the rousing, appreciative applause, I wondered, did these *teenagers* have any idea of the story they told?

At Omaha—another of the lonely beaches—John Mark and I walked down the steps from that high bluff, through the woods and sea grass, to the top of the beach. It was low tide. Blokarts--sailboats on wheels—flashed around on the sand flats near the water's edge in a refreshingly brisk, warm wind. Bruised, angry clouds scudded across a blue sky. When the sun emerged, it grew instantly hot. We walked barefoot all the way down that beach, past the high tide mark, through warm, shallow puddles, onto the soft bars of wet sand, all the way to the edge of the water. Someone had drawn a heart on the beach. This was as perfect a monument as any at this place.

"Can I go in?" John Mark asked.

My immediate inclination was to say no. It would be miserable for him (and me) if he were soaking wet the rest of the day. We had no towels, no change of clothes. I held my tongue as my brain raced like blokarts for an answer. Dads always want to say yes.

For reasons I do not know, my thoughts snagged on baptism. Such a messy sacrament. The water is often cold, usually inconvenient, anathema to drowsy, unsuspecting babies. Besides the recipient's forehead, water drips down the preacher's sleeve, splashes onto the floor. The baby sometimes cries. If the receiver is older, he gets a bigger handful on his head and water sheets down his face camouflaging the tears that sometimes accompany the moment. The name of the Trinity is invoked. It is an intimate moment, a thin space. The minister makes the sign of the cross with her thumb on his forehead. A threshold is being crossed. "The old life is gone," holy writ announces. "The new life has begun." The congregation makes vows to support and nurture the baptized and his family, to teach, tend the nursery, give generously of time, talent, and treasure, be available at every stage of life until death itself makes the sacrament complete.

John Mark's distant voice brought me back to the moment. *"Can I?"*

"Of course you can," I heard myself say. "Why not?"

What can be more refreshing? What could be a more grievous waste than standing by the ocean and not jumping in? He waded in up to his knees. His wide eyes and lips puckered in an emphatic "O" told me the water was frigid. He thought better of diving in and trotted out to my side. Together we watched the water for a long moment without speaking, then we looked behind us, back up the beach to the high bluffs. Nearly three thousand men were slaughtered trying to get from this heart drawn in the sand to the top of the beach. It was a distance of maybe 300 yards that felt like forever.

It was muggy and hot. The sun broiled. Big clouds huddled on the horizon plotting a late-afternoon deluge. As we headed back up to the path through the cattails, up the bluff, I loaded my pockets with small, rounded stones as keepsakes. This was probably illegal, but they would help me remember, and forgetting would be a moral failure. We joined Benjamin, Joseph, and Rachel on the bluff where they had been slowly walking through the graveyard. It was an impossible place. All the death arranged in such perfect lines of marble markers. The average age of the 9,387 dead was twenty-four.

The tragic coast of Normandy, particularly this cemetery (and others we didn't tour), is a looking-back place, a place that bears witness. We have heard our fathers' and brothers' screams, and we have glimpsed them running for cover on this bluff. We want to open our arms for them, to shelter them. But we cannot. We cannot save them from the slaughter. Nor can we comfort them. We can do nothing but remember, return home, tell what we saw, and hope that it's not too late to shelter others with what we've learned, from what we've seen. Compared to the battlefields in Belgium, the war came into more vivid relief at this cemetery. Those crosses and stars of David told the story without saying a word.

My knees weakened. I wanted to sit down. It had gotten even hotter. My boys strode up the walk back to the bus, shoving each other around, laughing. They didn't look cynical or naïve. They just looked young. And, thank God for it, they looked happy.

Our lumbering bus could barely fit onto the winding, narrow roads that twisted through fields, orchards, and coastal towns like Longues-sue-Mer. From my window seat I drank in the countryside turning golden in the late sun. We would be back in Paris by nine o'clock.

Caen had been rebuilt. Battlefields sprouted summer corn. The seaside resort at Juno, where the Canadians landed, was a destination for vacationing Parisians eager to get out of the city for a weekend. There was a small boat harbor filled with sailboats with names like *C'est La Vie*. Seaside villages dotted the cliffs to the north. Rachel said to me, "Let's come back *here* sometime. Just you and me."

Our guide spoke pretty good English, but it was drenched in such a pronounced French accent that I had to listen carefully to understand everything he said over the bus' PA system. His subjects and verbs didn't always agree. Some words in his care had picked up an added syllable. He was trying hard. I so appreciated his effort and was glad for his gentle nature and humor.

He added little, "yes, yeses" at the end of his paragraphs. I suspected these tics bought him time to translate in his head the next thing he wanted to say. He told us that eighty percent of all apples eaten in Europe come from Normandy. Life bursts from this place once so marred by death. I thirsted for the apple juice and ciders that he praised. I wanted to sink my teeth into a local, crisp apple right off a tree. *Calvados*, he opined, was an apple liqueur with the kick of a mule. "We drink it between courses, as it clears the palate, yes, yes? We cook with it. We drink it while we cook." Passengers laughed. "We call it—how-you-say?—a digestif. It puts a hole in the middle of your stomach, yes, yes?" We laughed again.

"Just enjoy the scene-*ary*," he said lyrically. "Soon we will stop for a *dee*-nar." He clicked off his microphone.

I enjoyed the silence.

Edith Shain died in her home in Los Angeles at 91. She claimed to be the nurse whom a sailor kissed in Times Square captured in the iconic *Life Magazine* photo marking the end of WWII. He has swept her forcefully into his young arms. He leans in and she leans back when he plants a big kiss on her lips as *Life* photographer Alfred Eisenstaedt froze the moment on film. He never got the names of the sailor and nurse.

In an interview later in life, Shain said, "[A]s for the picture, it says so many things — hope, love, peace and tomorrow."[28]

I thought we had come to Normandy to get a taste of an important part of our past. We wanted our boys to learn about and remember that past. But this trip wasn't about the past, after all.

This trip was about *tomorrow.*

10

A Perfect View

Like Mark Twain, when I saw the neatly arranged buildings and manicured grounds of Versailles, I wondered if I had been duped into an exquisite dream. Fences, globbed in gold, surrounded the palace and their thick iron palings ended in sharp feurs-de-lis. If you climbed those babies and slipped you'd be the perfect shish kebab—or one of Louis XIV's roast pigs. Below the palace in the back are the gardens lined with beds of blooming flowers, impeccably groomed and fancifully shaped shrubs, and fountains springing forth jets of water from statuary lips. My sons enjoyed the larger than life marble statues lining the gardens, particularly those of naked persons striking ridiculous poses. A snake suckling Cleopatra's right breast was a big hit.

Tourists crammed the place. The palace rooms had no air conditioning. Floor to ceiling windows stood wide open, which created a modest movement of air: the hot, stale air from the inside exchanged with the hot, humid air on the outside. These spacious rooms were stuffy enough in the afternoon heat without these perspiring legions. Four busloads of Brits packed one room. Jammed in another room, the whole population of China stood on each other's toes. And mine. All I could easily glimpse were the ornate ceilings. I could smell what people had for lunch—the garlic, the burgers, the eel. Not everyone's deodorant was working—probably mine included. We smelled a little like leather, wet earth from a deep hole, and male teenagers in a fart contest an hour after an Austin dinner of authentic Tex-Mex. *Really.*

Our boys and I made a game out of pushing through the gridlocked crowds as quickly as possible without causing a stampede. We bumped politely into and rubbed against purses, hips, clunky cameras, mashed breasts, bellies soaked with yellowish sweat, shoulders, elbows, silver belt buckles, outlandish buttocks. The boys had charted a course on the other side of the room. The younger two followed Joseph who, at six-feet tall, could see over many heads and squirm his way through the holes and gaps. I—still wiser than my children—was better at anticipating where crevasses would split open. We slid through the crowd as quickly as we could without leaving behind a wake of elderly visitors sprawled on the floor.

The displays in the great halls that I could actually see underscored the nuance between power and authority. The powerful stand, conveying a brute strength. A seated position of authority, so it is explained, confers a more serene public charge upon the sitter. The one is muscles the other magisterial.

My father had a clear understanding of parental power. He didn't want any. "Ask your mother," was his way of saying, "I make the money not the decisions." The best way to avoid conflict is to keep your dog out of the fight.

My theology kept getting the better of me as I took in this ostentatious royal residence. Real power comes from kneeling to serve people less fortunate than you—loving best the ones who hurt most. And monarchy, or what my old minister once called a benevolent dictatorship, is reserved for God.

Rachel and I caught up with our sons in the fresh air. The air outside was still hot, but it didn't smell so *used.* They had beat us to the front lawn by a full five minutes. I asked John Mark what stood out.

"A whole lot of naked people," he said, referring to the garden statuary.

"What about the inside?" I asked, hoping for something more apropos for a place of such history and culture.

"A whole lot more naked people."

When pushed, he said the palace was such a big, golden space. *We're getting somewhere,* I thought. But most impressive, he reported, was all the umbrellas stacked every which way in a lost and found room that I never saw and into which he had accidentally stumbled, awestruck. If he wrote a what-I-did-this-summer paper for school, hopefully he'd make classier observations. Or not.

A performance artist dressed as King Tut presided over a clutch of Africans who hawked scarves, Eiffel Tower key chains and earrings, and styrofoam airplanes shaped like birds, which they launched in an endless succession of graceful mid-air swoops and climbs. Every now and then some poor tourist got bonked in the head by these rubber-band propelled birds, a bargain at nearly whatever price you wanted to offer. Having never seen the likes of Disney World, King Louis XIV would have been confounded.

When we got back to Paris, we stopped to gawk at the real Eiffel Tower. The beggars ignored my family and everyone else on the street, but they zeroed in on me. Something about my face said sucker. They sidled up to me with irresistibly sad eyes and the polish of people who did this for a living.

One woman presented a note written in English stating her kids had a genetic disease. The content got my attention almost as much as the neatly penciled cursive. Another woman insisted I help a colony of deaf children. Memo to self: increase my giving to my local church where we actually *exist* to make a difference in the world. I reminded myself that we contributed more than a few euros to the offering at the American Church in Paris. But as usual, I felt heartless for saying no to these skilled, unctuous women.

I also made a mental note never to count on my family. Instead of coming to my rescue, I noticed them in my peripheral vision heading off to take more photographs of the tower. I extricated myself without their help.

From any angle, the Eiffel Tower is formidable. Some hated it when it was constructed for the 1889 World Fair, calling it "the odious shadow of the odious column built up of riveted iron plates."[29] Detractors—including short story writer Guy de Maupassant—were known to routinely eat lunch in its restaurant; at least when you're on it, they reasoned, you didn't have to look at it.

Benjamin, Joseph, and Rachel—queasy about heights and warier of the ticket lines that stretched to Oklahoma—headed back to the apartment to make dinner. Against my better judgment, John Mark and I got in line. I began psyching myself up for the trip to the top. None in my family is as afraid of heights as I am.

"Long line," John Mark remarked. "But it isn't as long as the Intimidator at Carowinds."

Carowinds is an amusement park near Charlotte, North Carolina, filled with terrifying things they call "rides." Roller coasters and tilt-a-wheels there are meant to cause week-long nausea. Cokes and burgers there require an outlay of money akin to a house payment. I dread places like that, and I was beginning all the more to fear the ride on the glass elevator up to the top of this tower, which from directly underneath seems to rise to the moon.

My heart began to race.

John Mark sensed I was petrified. He asked, "Are you scared to go up, Dad?"

I said, "Yes."

"I thought so," he said smugly.

I wondered why I didn't just step out of line and go back to our apartment. I could tell John Mark that my fear got the best of me. I could tell him I was coming down with an aneurism. I didn't have to go through with this. I had nothing to prove. So what? I'm claustrophobic and afraid of places any higher above sea level than a step stool. The manly thing to do, I reasoned, was to admit my fears to my son so that he could learn how one could face scary things. If I got to the top without passing out, he would learn perseverance. If I died ingloriously from a sweating panic attack in line, he would know that I was at least trying to be courageous, and, more importantly, I didn't let my fears sideline me.

I explained to him that I was trying to get into my zone, trying to talk myself out of the terror that seized me.

"Oh," he said with a devilish detachment. "Get over it."

What a punk. But I could not be angry because he was so happy to be so annoyingly under my skin.

"Did Pops have to be brave?" he asked.

This was a curve ball. I thought about that. Of course he had to be brave. Sleeping in a hole, fighting, getting shot at, the fear of the unknown, being a prisoner of war. He had to be very brave.

"I guess he had to be brave," I said. "He and I never actually talked about that."

"Was he brave enough to climb to the top of the Eiffel Tower after the war?"

It made me wonder. Could a man who was shot at and had tasted starvation still fear a simple elevator ride to the top of a very tall tower on a sunny day?

I used the time waiting in line to reflect on our trip so far. How were these travels and our time together shaping my sons? What were they learning? Surely, they were taking more in then they let on. Benjamin asked me to stand by a cornfield between Pointe de Huc and the bus parking lot. He wanted to take my picture. He carefully framed the shot. He instructed me to look out onto the field. New corn was coming in. I pointed to the lines of trees and shrubs on the low hills that formed a boundary around that rectangular field. I told him that that ridge of trees was called a hedgerow and that soldiers had to take one hedgerow at a time, and eventually charge across or around each of those open fields. Often, fields just like this one were mined. It was slow, deadly going.

"*I know*," Ben insisted.

He looked at me like I had just been hit in the head with a board. He had read about hedgerows in the museum at Caen. From his seat in the back of the van, he had heard Martin mention them in the hills above Bastogne. He had been paying attention. His practiced teen indifference was a sophisticated ruse that he had been perfecting at Riverside Middle School.

On October 21, 1944, Hitler personally briefed SS Obersturmbannfuhrer Otto Skorzeny about the role he would later play in the Battle of the Bulge. Skorzeny, a successful commando leader, was to recruit English-speaking German soldiers to form the 150th Panzer Brigade. In American uniforms, they were to infiltrate the American line in American jeeps prior to the German attack. Behind the lines, they cut telephone wires, misdirected traffic, and "even made it to the Meuse."[30] Dad remembered them—clean cut guys whose English was too perfect, whose faces too closely shaved, and whose uniforms too pristine. Most were captured immediately, and some were executed on the battle front as spies. They looked like everybody else, they spoke the language, they wore the same clothes, but they didn't belong.

Every teenager knows the feeling. Teens act like they fit into classes that are over their heads, act like the adult world all around them makes sense when it's absurd. They try to fit in. They try to belong. They assume the guise.

Part of Ben's mask nowadays includes being careful about smiling. Braces may be one reason why. But a smile reveals his dimple. And when he smiles you know he's a sweet kid. When his mask is in place, he could pass as a brooding tough guy. When he smiles, he oozes sugar.

When I was growing up, the guise came with a uniform: Levi straight leg cords. Every cool guy wore them. Even if you weren't cool, if you wore the cords at least you didn't draw attention to yourself. My friends and I were experts at doing what we had to do to fit in. We pretended to be Hampton High School's three musketeers. Every girl recognized our truer affinity to the Three Stooges.

Even now sometimes I feel like an imposter. Because I don't wear a clerical collar, strangers don't automatically know I'm a minister. But when they find out, I can almost feel them put me into a pigeonhole. Until I speak up, I become their version of me: a teetotaler; a speaker of tongues; a milquetoast do-gooder; a segregationist homophobe; an anything goes liberal. In fact, I'm none of those things. The masks others want me to wear don't fit. That is not to say I don't have a closet full of costumes, sans clerical collar.

Despite my best efforts to come off as keenly intelligent, clownish, and laidback, I often feel like a dolt. I use humor to keep scary things at bay. And I am routinely nervous about what people will think if they discover the real me. Like Skorzeny's spies, sometimes it's easier being someone you're not. Being yourself takes courage. If you wear a mask, you always have to ask, what mask do I wear today? with this group? in this setting? The danger is that you've already lost yourself.

Surely my sons never feel like that. They've got it together in ways I never had. Aren't my guys immune to this part of growing up? Joseph is getting ready for college. Benjamin starts high school. What are they discovering about themselves, their *true* selves? What do they look like when they aren't posturing, putting on a face, wearing a mask? What kind of men will they become? What kind of fathers? What kind of dad am I? You've got to be brave just to look honestly in the mirror.

And it's not just a struggle for teenagers. Their fathers struggle, too. Are all tourists beset by such thoughts waiting for the elevator at the Eifel Tower?

The ride to the top of the Eiffel Tower didn't kill me. In fact, the ride was exhilarating. It was cool at the top. There was no wind, not even a breeze. What a perfect view. John Mark and I traced the streets to our hotel. We pinpointed the Métro station by the Arc de Triumphe. We snapped pictures of each other, and asked others to take pictures of us. We used the restroom in the tiny bathroom at the center of the observation deck because taking a whiz seemed to be the very thing to do at the top of Paris' monstrous and now beloved tower. What a kick. We laughed so hard.

We dined on mediocre pizza from the cafeteria and made toasts with cherry Coke. We supplied the pigeons pinches of pizza dough. The sun was setting. We were thrilled to be at the top. I would be forever grateful that John Mark talked me into braving the long line and my even longer line of excuses to resist. I hoped that Dad was occasionally as happy with me as I was on the top of the Eiffel Tower with my intrepid youngest.

John Mark and I leaned over the rail a very long time. City lights winked on. I thought we might get lost finding our apartment through the dark passages snaking like veins through light. But getting home didn't matter at the moment. Standing here did. The winding, green Seine and still greener trees made the buildings stand out. The buildings and monuments glowed in the twilight, all of them white, like bones.

11

Neither Sighing

Dad came home from the war in one piece. He was repatriated by American troops from Germany on Friday the 13th of April. He knows nothing of where he was released from. His family would forever know the 13th as *Bill's Day*. It is no small irony that, 25 years later, his mother died on Friday the 13th of November. Dad's memory was fuzzy about a lot of things, but not about the day he was liberated from captivity. Nor did he forget that his first meal as a free man was fried eggs, which he devoured, then in a jeep heading to Paris immediately afterwards, he made the driver stop so he could vomit. It had been the richest food he'd eaten in four months. Dad weighed 100 pounds, down 44-pounds from his enlistment weight in February 1943.

There were no beds in the Paris hospital. He remembers being set down on a hallway floor lined shoulder-to-shoulder with other happy but weak-as-a-kitten liberated POWs. A smiling Red Cross nurse walked along one side of the corridor handing out D Ration chocolate bars intended to last the day; by the time she had returned down the other side of the hallway, Dad had eaten his bars. When he told that story—and

I heard that one often—he blinked back tears every time. Was it the hunger that drew tears with the remembering, or was it that woman's kindness, or was it that it was all, finally, over? He had dodged death, but had come close. Now there was life, a tile floor, chocolate, a pretty woman's legs, whimpering men no longer afraid of death but afraid, perhaps, of what they might yet become.

Medical bulletins in 1945 listed detailed precautions to be taken to protect former prisoners. These bulletins described how "RAMPs" (Recovered Allied Military Personnel) were to avoid *gastro-intestinal disturbances*. Restricted food included donuts, peanuts, citrus fruits, cauliflower, cabbage, the concentrated components of C and K-rations, and foods high in fat. The general mess should be on a soft or bland diet—the likes of dried pea soup, cheese sandwiches on white bread—both before and during the voyage home.[31]

On June 7, when he had gotten stronger, the Army flew him back to the states. An engine on the plane from Paris conked out twice. Both times they were an hour out and had to turn around. They made it to New York City where he caught a couple of innings of a Yankees game against the Red Sox; it was front row and all the free hot dogs convalescing GIs cared to eat, a far cry from the bland food in Paris. Baseball may have been more appealing to most GIs than the benefit concert for the United Negro College Fund on June 10 at Carnegie Hall featuring a 70-piece orchestra made up of workers from the Sperry Gyroscope Company. Slurping beer and rooting for a homerun with ducks on the pond might have been a healthier release for frazzled young men with so much pent up inside. Sometime later that month, the Army shipped Dad on a train to McGuire's VA Hospital in Richmond.

He was officially discharged on December 9th. According to his discharge papers, he had been in Europe seven months and eight days. Over half of that time he was a prisoner. For four days he was in the Battle of the Bulge.

Upon his arrival home, safe and mostly sound, he spent his back pay on a brand new double pedestal dining table for his mother. It had three leaves and could sit ten people.

In early 1947 he met Barbara Ann Burriss. They worked on the second floor at the National Advisory Committee for Aeronautics (NACA), the forerunner of NASA, at Langley Field—he at the rear in mechanical reproduction, she at the front as a copy editor in the technical illustration department. Mr. Nixon was their boss, the one who fired Dad for clocking out 15-minutes early one night.

In March of 1948 they married at First Presbyterian Church in Newport News. Mom's mother—who never condoned change—didn't bless these nuptials and almost didn't attend the ceremony. Mom and Dad are smiling in the picture taken of them outside on the threshold of the sanctuary after the service, but you can see the pinched stress in their faces, too. Mom wore a corsage of gardenias and Dad a single carnation. They received 59 wedding gifts. Mom kept record of each and wrote thank you notes for every one. Dad's Granny Parramore gave them a check for $15. J.P. Dale gave them a gravy ladle. Brother Jim Matthews and his new bride Ginny gave them a General Electric double waffle iron. Their total bill at checkout for three honeymoon nights at the Washington Duke Hotel in Durham was $31.01.

Dad left the Baptist church of his youth to join his wife's tribe, the Presbyterians. By 1953, they had two daughters, Susan Greer and Carol Ann. At various times, he sold Fuller brushes, worked at Red Wallace's electrical business, and laid tile for a company on Mercury Boulevard. When Dr. Noel Nelms, who delivered my sisters and me, told him that his knees couldn't stand the rigors of laying carpet and tile, Dad began working in a succession of furniture stores: Rountree, *Hampton's Progressive Home Furnishers;* Montgomery Ward; Brittingham; Bell; Wythe House; J.C. Penny; and back to Montgomery Ward after his heart bypass surgery in 1982.

In an era when many men went to work for one company and stayed until retirement, Dad's vocational restlessness stands out. Except for his NACA job, he was never fired. He was trusted with money and with opening and closing shop. By all accounts he worked hard, but he knew how to pace himself. While they were in high school, cousins Dave and Bruce Whitcomb worked part time with Dad at Brittingham.

Dave reports that Dad was fond of naps, and on late Tuesday afternoons when Dave would show up after school, he'd often find Dad *testing* one of the recliners.

It's a good chance his experience as a war prisoner figured into this vocational impatience. He was free to hop jobs, so he simply did. Maybe job changes didn't faze him because he faced down bigger tests long ago, and his biggest worries ended on April 13, 1945.

As with so many of my speculations, he never told me. And I'll never know.

For a time in the mid-1950's he worked three jobs at once to make ends meet. When he worked in the mold loft at Newport News Shipyard, an accident in 1962 crushed a leg; that put him out of work for seven months. A young Rev. Andrews came over one Sunday night and asked Mom to step outside with him. There, in the front yard, he pulled from his suit jacket pocket wads of cash. A collection was taken during worship that night at their church.

"I can't take this," she protested.

"You *have* to take this," he explained. "Your friends need to help your family, and you need to let them."

The money was a godsend. My mother learned on that front lawn that a gift has two parts, the giving and receiving. Rev. Andrews, always the teacher, underscored for my shocked mom both the need to give, which was no surprise to her generous heart, and the need to take. This rendered my weeping mother speechless. Those friends needed to give, and she needed to let them. Ask my mother the meaning of the word grace and this is the story you will get.

I was a surprise in 1964—born in Hampton General Hospital twenty years after Dad crossed the Atlantic bound for WWII. Both of my sisters were married and gone by the time I was in first grade. I had a working class dad and a stay-at-home mom all to myself.

Dad was a self-described jack-of-all trades and master of none. I learned by watching him work, though my impatience as a student matched his impatience as a teacher. One lesson I learned early and well was to avoid roofs.

When I was six, Dad toppled off our garage roof. Louis Crockett our back door neighbor who drove tankers for Esso handled the job on the ground hoisting up the shingles. Dad slapped them on the felted deck in nearly straight courses and tacked them down rapid fire despite the gale that pasted back his hair and tore at his clothes. He worked his way up to the precarious peak. I watched distractedly from the backyard; I was waiting for the fireflies; unwilling to brave the wind, they never showed up. One minute Dad was silhouetted against the dusk, the next he skidded down with only a single, high pitched yelp, flopping appendages digging uselessly into asphalt shingles for traction. Perfect silence stilled the roiled air as he cleared the eaves and nosedived towards earth. It was this moment that was the most exquisite. A solid thud followed like an exclamation point, or at least a colon. Then a sound from within him oozed out: an involuntary, hissing rush of rubbery air.

He got up after a long moment with some difficulty. I'd seen cowboys get up like that after a punch in a bar fight. He tested his balance and gingerly wiggled his body parts one by one—knuckles, knees, jaw. He paced a slow circle around the impression his body stamped into the ground. It was a wonder, I thought. No other dad in the neighborhood could have pulled that off like *mine*. It was better than the circus. But I remember feeling a little disappointed that the fall didn't kill him because it would have been such a spectacular way to go. Plus, I would have gotten such sympathy from my peers at show and tell in Mrs. Lingenfelder's half-day kindergarten class who all, I presumed, had living fathers.

As long as I can remember, my mom lamented that Dad was afflicted with *Parramore Skin*. It was delicate, Mom would say. Paper thin, like his mother's. I remember Grandmother Matthews only from fading Christmas pictures and her skin looks decidedly normal in the Polaroids. But Dad would come home from one of his trips to the hospital in his wheezing, elder years brandishing one or both arms that sported glorious, purple-green bruises from IVs. It was another sterling example of familial epidermis minimus. As a younger man sunburn would get him, or an irritating loose thread from a shirt collar might tickle him nearly to death, or the hungry teeth of one of his ripsaws in his shop might nip some flesh. Mom would clean up the wound. He'd wince but never complain. She'd make some pronouncement about how he needed to be more careful. Needed to take better care of his you-know-what.

Like most sons, I believed deep in my soft heart that my dad was made of steel and coiled wire. He would live forever. He shook off that slow-motion fall from the roof. I was frozen in the middle of the yard. Mom flew to him from the patio. Coming to himself, he smiled sheepishly at her. She gave him a stern once-over while he muttered that he was just fine. Just a few scratches. An elbow was slick with blood. The knee of his pants, also spotted with blood, was ripped out. But everything seemed to function. No fuss necessary. I'm sure he muttered something like, 'Gotta get the rest of these shingles on before dark. Before the coming rain.' Before he bleeds to death, is what I was thinking, what with his thin skin.

A child doesn't understand a lot of things, like why his brave, strong mother comes into the dark house and melts into sobs after her husband gets back on the roof. And this skin thing completely flummoxed me. On days when he wasn't falling off roofs, Dad looked fine to me. He was fair and had some freckling. His arms and legs didn't have much hair on them, but he had a small grey nest of it in the center of his chest. Besides being a little older than the rest, he looked like every other father, more or less.

Nor did I understand the function of oral tradition, about how family stories get spun to a finer, higher shine until they identify a people and sew together generations. There was the time Dad's Granny ate a whole box of cookies without knowing they were actually dog biscuits. There's the one about Uncle Jim getting shot at with a pistol on the Boulevard by a classmate, and the time during the Depression when neighborhood boys got the watchman drunk and stole the wood he was guarding at a new house in order that they might build a raft on Indian River Creek. Our extended family has often gabbed about the oddities of our immediate ancestors' Virginia speech; when somebody pipes in, "There's a mowse in the howse; better let him owt" we all laugh. I've heard comment about the Matthews' big lips and small but strong hands. And, of course, whenever Mom or one of the aunts mentioned that Parramore skin, it drew lots of smiling nods, as if to say, *Yes, we're such a delicate people.*

Those generous lips and the stories that still make us snort were among the raw materials that made my father. He possessed those contradictory strong hands and that thin skin, which on a metaphorical level probably explains a lot. But as a kid I didn't get it. The young Matt Matthews simply held him in awe.

My respect for Dad had limits. In second grade we built a rowboat together. We worked in the garage late into the evenings. I got to hold the boards, and he got to use the screwdriver. Why couldn't *he* hold the boards and *I* use the screwdriver? When I got to try turning the impossible screws into the unyielding plywood, why couldn't I use a hammer? Wouldn't a hammer be quicker? How come I had to hold the light and not the saw? And why did he waste his breath telling me what to do? I wasn't stupid. I could figure it out. And why was he yelling at me? And why was I yelling at him? How come we measured twice and cut once? That took too much time. Who cared about what a right angle was? He called it *geometry*, but what could geometry possibly have to do with rowboats? What did he mean when he said you got to let the tool do the work for you, that you can't force things? And how come the wood needed to be primed before painted? And when were we going to get that boat into the water already?

Before a nor'easter washed that boat and part of our pier away years later, I spent many sunny hours rowing it up and down Indian River Creek. Soon, I could feather the oars and pull across the shallow flats without a ripple. The herons stalking fish in the nearby marsh began to pay me no mind. I landed on tiny Duck Island and strode upon it like Captain John Smith reconnoitering the Strawberry Banks or like Blackbeard calmly taking charge of another captured frigate. I was Tom Sawyer on the Mississippi and Neil Armstrong on the moon. My dad had done the same thing—in that same creek—when he was a kid.

The hours constructing that skiff from sheets of inexpensive plywood were trying—for both of us. Life isn't just one or two photographs of posed, happy scenes. Sometimes there is the dust of battle. Sometimes fathers and sons make sparks.

When that nor'easter sucked our rowboat forever away, Dad and I both missed it. But neither of us suggested building another one. We might not have survived.

'Home' for Dad was his castle, and Mom was the homemaker. She was the emotional center. The saying held true in their household: If mom isn't happy, nobody's happy. If dad isn't happy, nobody notices. Mom paid the bills and managed the money. She cooked three square meals of slow food each day. She washed dishes. She vacuumed. She made and mended clothes. When I skinned a knee, I went to her.

Dad did what men of his generation were expected to do. By the time I came along he was finally able to bring home steady income. Besides fixing things that broke, his domestic chores were limited, meaning he didn't have any as far as I could tell. No house cleaning. No cooking. No helping with homework. He didn't even cut the grass until he retired. Mom did it.

His fathering duties were light, but he did give parenting some effort. While he never changed a diaper, when I was in first grade, he and I joined some father-son club akin to cub scouts. He was Big Cloud. I was Little Cloud. Our association with that group didn't last much beyond a campfire but we made leather nametags that we wore around our necks on a lanyard. I still think that was pretty cool.

Later that year, after saving up money for eons, we went to see my Mom's much-loved brother in Burbank. Uncle Bob wore mod sunglasses and worked for Warner Brothers. Mom and I flew out alone for the first week; Dad was to join us for the second. As we made a bumpy descent into LAX, I gripped the armrests with all my might. I had never flown and was petrified. As we descended heavily to earth, I thought we were goners. I pleaded with God for a miracle.

"I wish Dad was here," I told Mom through gritted teeth.

She leaned close and spoke into my ear. "He'll be here next week, honey."

I winced every time the plane lurched and bobbled, every time the plastic creaked, and unseen gears, rods, and flaps shrieked and popped. The ground was rising up to meet us like a concrete punch.

"But I wish he was here *now*," I whimpered.

"Why?" Mom asked.

"'Cause we might crash," I said. *Duh*.

"There's nothing he could do if he were here."

My fear went away immediately. I glared at her. I couldn't believe what she'd said. If Dad were here, we wouldn't crash. *That's what dad's do*. How did she not know that dad's make everything better? At least *mine* did. Until the day he died, part of me always believed that. Fathers have such power.

We picked him up at the airport one week later. He had a week's pay rolled up in either shoe, which explained why he stood a little taller than usual.

Dad had the gift of gab. For most of my childhood he sold furniture and appliances at J.C. Penny. When I was old enough to hang out at the Coliseum Mall alone while Mom shopped, I'd find my way upstairs to the furniture department at Penny to check on my old man. I watched him welcome customers to the floor. He introduced himself, asked them what he could do to help them. If they gave him an opening, he'd get around to talking about where they were from and what they did for a living. He'd ask about their last name, their people. Did they have kids? He could chat it up a long time without mentioning recliners and water dispensers on new refrigerator models. He was curious about people.

He was barred from the managerial ranks because he didn't have a college degree. Being on the floor while not being responsible for the floor probably suited him fine. Over dinner at home, I remember him occasionally griping to my Mom about the way it ought to be at the store. But he was glad not to have to be responsible for doing it. He never had patience with bureaucracy. When customers stepped off the escalator, though, he was in charge and they were in good hands.

Once I followed him around as he strolled with a young couple to the appliances lined along the hallway by the elevators. He listened to what they wanted. Amazingly, he told them that what JC Penny had to offer probably wouldn't suit them as well as a Montgomery Ward brand. They thanked him. Both of them shook his hand. Even as a kid, I knew he might have gotten the sale had he not mentioned a competitor. But for Dad, the sale wasn't the main thing. I don't think his referral was a calculated ploy to get them to come back when they needed a couch. It was his way of treating people right.

I watched and learned. The way he connected with people was perhaps his greatest gift to me. I love chatting it up with people, just like he did. I'm not as gregarious as my father, maybe, but when I'm visiting with somebody I can almost feel Dad's curiosity about others tingling to life within me. Like him, I care for the people I meet on the job.

During my senior year of high school, Dad's second heart attack was prelude to early retirement. When he got back on his feet, working in the garage took up a lot of his time. He made furniture for family and friends. He often kept a garden; one year it was half the size of our large backyard. The next year it was slightly larger than Tennessee. He grew a forest of corn, tomatoes, Swiss chard, and an almost endless supply of string beans. He helped neighbors with chores that needed an extra hand. He cut grass at church and met contractors there when repairs were being made. He loved to listen to my sister play piano and sing. He routinely got teary at sad movies. He wouldn't argue politics or religion with anybody. He liked a good hand of bridge, and I regret like crazy that I never learned to play. He enjoyed his siblings. He liked to hear about other people's successes; his genuine happiness for them usually overshadowed his envy, which ran deep. He generally didn't stick around for bad news. Mom and Dad planted the yard with azaleas and flowers. She'd weed. He'd loop a chain from the chrome bumper of the family car to the trunks of the shrubs that didn't make it, and how I loved to watch him spin the tires.

My parents' home was immaculate. Their yard belonged on a magazine cover. I admire the way my parents made a life and a home.

Dad always taught me that the best part of any trip was coming home. In his later years, he came home from stays at Hampton General Hospital or, more frequently, from the Hampton VA Medical Center, a bit more battered and diminished each time, but just as glad to shuffle over the threshold from the porch to their cheery kitchen. And no matter how tired or late, he'd always go the few extra blocks out of his way to drive down Chesapeake Avenue. He called it the scenic route, or, simply, the Boulevard. Seeing the harbor and smelling the salt air meant he'd arrived, and to no small degree, all was right with the world. At night, seeing the distant, colored lights of Norfolk on the other side of the harbor stretched out like Christmas made homecoming all the sweeter.

Dad and I loved our hometown, but this idyllic waterfront has run with blood and prejudice. As early as 1609, Indians on the peninsula had been both courted by settlers and attacked. Hampton was called Elizabeth City in 1621 when Rev. Jonas Stockton wrote of the "treacherous character"[32] of the Indians and appeared to be an early proponent of the doctrine that the only good Indian was a dead Indian. Had Mr. Stockton already forgotten how the Powhatan Confederacy— some say as large as 300 wigwams and nearly one thousand Kecoughtans, Chesapeakes, Algonquin and other Tidewater tribes—had provisioned the London Company's larders? Captain John Smith had traded them glass beads in return. "We were never more merry nor fed on more plenty of good oysters, fish, flesh, and wild fowle and good breade, nor never had better fires in England than in the dry smoky houses of Kecoughtan."[33]

Expansionist swagger created tension between settlers and the settled upon. In the Indian Rebellion of March of 1622, Powhatan slaughtered 346 of the 1,240 white inhabitants.

Our home town was a tough place. In 1717, Captain Henry Maynard sailed into Hampton River swinging Edward Teach's severed head at the bowsprit. He fixed it on a pole at the entrance of Sunset Creek, and that point is still known by history buffs as Blackbeard Point.

When the British approached in 1812, Hamptonians burned their own city to the ground rather then let the redcoats capture it. Virginia Rebels applied the torch again in 1861 at the beginning of the Civil War when Unionists brought reinforcements to Fort Monroe; better to give the Union ashes than an actual town to capture. Confederate General John B. MacGruder, tasked with defending Richmond from the east, gave the residents 15 minutes to pack their things before the Old Dominion Dragoons set some thirty buildings and 100 homes alight, including the Hampton Baptist Church which my father's family was to call home for nearly a century.

Dad and I came from a town that had known more than just sleepy peace. Beneath the nighttime lights across the harbor that he and I loved looking at were rows and rows of nuclear-powered warships ready at a moment's notice to flex American muscle anywhere in the world.

On Dad's last visit to the fifth floor of the Hampton VA Medical Center, which overlooked the harbor from the mouth of Hampton River, he told Mom, "I want to go home." Oxygen and the steroids eased his wheezing, but made his voice high and squeaky.

Mom and I had been frantically shopping nursing homes, trying to find a place for him to go upon discharge. The hospital couldn't do anything more for him; his COPD wasn't going to get better and there was no way Mom could take care of him at home. His breathing had become too labored, he was too unsteady on his feet, and he had begun to get loopy-headed. The best places had no vacancy. The VA hospice would have been ideal: good care, fifteen minutes away from

Mom, but most of all, an unobstructed view of the harbor he loved. But there was no room.

We were not surprised when he died, but we were shocked. I had never before, or have I since, experienced the depth of numbness I felt when we got the news. Rachel and I had stopped by their house to pick Mom up for the short drive to the hospital. It was Epiphany Sunday. Mom got the phone call as we were walking out the door. Dad was gone. The nurse on the other end of that clear line said, simply, that he had "passed away." Mom nearly went to her knees.

We were ready, but we weren't ready. I made a few immediate phone calls to make arrangements for our children's care that afternoon. Our plans for childcare and for work were engulfed by a swollen river filled with bobbing deck chairs and lost rowboats and old logs from the drowned banks. Racing water swept away lawns and submerged low bridges. I had been with dozens of families at the moment of a loved one's death, and I was the first to arrive to dozens more after the accident, after the code was called, after the nearest of kin were notified. I knew what to do, but I didn't know what to do when it came to the death of my own father. I was emotionally okay, but I was not okay, for I was adrift. We were expecting this, but we weren't. I knew how to ride the waves of this swelling tide—at least I thought I did—and never once did I worry about slipping beneath the water; but I could never have predicted how powerful the rush was, how strong, untamable, raw, and unkind.

We exchanged confused hugs: I hugged Mom, Rachel hugged Mom, I hugged Rachel, Rachel hugged Mom again. With white-face, painted-on frowns, and foam noses, we could have passed as awkward clowns at the circus. Mom said, "O God." We hugged again. We wept a little; but it was not the tears that came out that I noticed, it was the tears dammed inside. Those damned tears. There was much that would need to be done, but for now, since we had been on our way out anyway, we needed only to get to the hospital to see him— his body—one last time. I had driven to the VA many times, but never not to be greeted by my dad's glad smile. I jangled my keys, absently herding Mom and Rachel to the car. This couldn't be happening, but it was.

The nurses gave us privacy. We collected his scant belongings and literally gawked at his lifeless form. He was altogether there, but completely absent; so physically present but otherwise so oddly *passed away*. Mom looked out his window. Recent, and rare, snow melted into the wirey lawn. The harbor danced with slants of bright, late afternoon light. "Give rest, O Christ," says the prayer book. "Give rest to thy servant with thy saints, where sorrow and pain are no more, neither sighing."

Days before, Mom had taken home his valuables. Watches and wallets go missing in hospitals. Now, there was very little of him left to take home. No clothes, no shoes, no reading glasses or other detritus on the bedside table. I wondered if we should keep his dentures. They were all that was left, those plastic choppers that he'd pop out of his head while he held our delighted little boys on his lap. They'd try to grab them, but he was too quick, sucking them back in place with a supersonic slurp. It was a fun, silly game when the boys were young. Now they were there for the taking. I absentmindedly checked below the sheets. His hospital gown had no pockets. There was nothing but him: pale, smooth thighs; a belly made plump with steroids; those garish, yellow toe nails. Like checking the closet and beneath the bed at a hotel room before check out, I didn't want to leave anything behind. Except I was going to leave him behind. I've never felt so empty handed.

"He said he wanted to go home," Mom remembered, looking out that window. "And now he is."

Heaven was fine enough a place for Pops. God knows how badly he needed the rest. But Alleghany Road, as far as Dad was concerned, would have been close enough. As long as you are near and, ideally, can see and smell the water, no sorrow or pain can leave you troubled for long. The sight of wind and light on the water does that to a person. It leaves you feeling easy, no pain, no trouble, not for long. *Neither sighing.*

We drove home very slowly. Whatever talking we were doing about making plans ceased when we got to the

Boulevard. I had taken the long way, of course. And we drove the last blocks home in silence.

12

Making Full Use of the Platform and Minding the Gap

Leaving Paris for London, we clicked like old pros through turnstiles, operated Métro machines, located the right hallways, levels, and tracks and settled on the 9031 to St. Pancras—the cathedral of the railways. She sailed above the outer arrondissements of Paris, picking up speed like a space ship, and whisked us away from a place I didn't want to leave. Picture-perfect countryside flashed by at 186-miles-per-hour. Plush carpets of buttery wheat waved among a dozen shades of green, the green of granny smith apples, worn money, limes, frozen peas, iguanas, street lights, the green of envy. Leaves on trees lining the tracks coyly revealed their dainty silver undersides like dancers at a cabaret who know better or little girls in a playground sandbox who don't.

I could get used to passenger trains—despite their being nearly extinct in the States. Large windows grabbed the world frame by blurring frame. It was easy to daydream. Dad liked to sing the song "I've been working on the railroad." I loved singing it with him while he drove me home from tennis practice. That soundtrack played in my mind accompanied by the harmony of metal wheels and the movement of hundreds of mechanical guts keeping perfect time. I heard Dinah Shore sing that song once, perhaps on her TV show. She had such a smooth voice and, thinking back on it, was easy on the eyes. The movement of both the car and of memory felt like time travel. I was not fighting anybody for an armrest. I dozed.

On the January afternoon after Dad's funeral service in 2002, an elderly woman offered me her hand during the reception. She spoke as if I should have known who she was but I couldn't place her faintly familiar face. Thankfully, she introduced herself. She was Mary Virginia Strup. Her maiden name, she said, was Peake. *Mary Virginia Peake!* I had heard that name routinely whenever the Hampton regulars and Dad's Wythe neighbors were discussed. I received her delicate, extended hand.

"We really loved Billy Boy," she said. "We worried about all the neighborhood boys going off to war."

The room was bright and loud as hungry mourners clattered around tables the church ladies had laden with meatballs and chunks of out-of-season melon from Chile. Sue Johnson had contributed a platter of her homemade eggrolls. Mary Lane and a dozen other women had decorated the room with flowers and framed pictures of Dad. Pimento cheese sandwiches were cut into triangles. Crab dip and crackers. A vegetable tray of radishes, carrots, and celery. It was a Tidewater, Virginia, spread of *church food.*

The one o'clock funeral had not run long, but the gathered had most probably missed lunch. I was starving. We had prayed, listened, remembered, and wept. We had sung the traditional *For All the Saints*, and one of Dad's favorite hymns, a relatively new one from the 1980's, that I also loved. I opened my mouth but the words would not come. The people packed in the pews around me sang, though. They stood in the aisles and spilled out the back doors. Their voices were a strong, solid thing.

I the Lord of sea and sky,

I have heard my people cry . . .

Pinched by hunger, we were now ready to eat. Clotted in small groups in the fellowship hall, family friends and strangers balanced tiny plastic plates mounded with Virginia ham biscuits in one hand and sweet iced tea in the other. Seated like Roosevelt at Yalta, Uncle Jim and other elderly people received visitors who leaned over them and shook their hands. Everyone chewed and talked at the same time, shouting to be heard. The crowd milled around visiting, and they laughed and laughed. It was like a dance. Dad would have loved it.

I wanted to ask this gentle woman—*Mary Virginia*—with the halo of wispy white hair to speak up, but I didn't dare. I still held her frail hand. She would not let go. She either couldn't speak very loudly, or couldn't say *this* very loudly. Some memories have to be whispered, or, like birds easily spooked, they scatter in a feathery blur.

She had dreamed of my father the night before she learned he was missing in action. A Western Union telegram from the Adjutant General of the US Army delivered news to Dad's folks in Hampton, and the Matthewes had gotten word to Dad's sisters, including Angeline at Madison College where she and Mary Virginia were learning to be teachers. Newspaper reports came later blackened with wire reports of what would be Hitler's last offensive. Aunt Mary Louise was in Philly where her husband was stationed.

Cy Peterman of the *Philadelphia Inquirer* would report that the 106th was "the worst-smacked and heaviest loser of all American units in front of Field Marshal von Rundstedt's counter-offensive in Belgium."[34] The *Stars & Stripes* later reported that it had been Belgium's coldest winter in forty years.[35] All the Wythe girls and families read about the cold and danger.

It was cold in the Shenandoah Valley, too, but a lot warmer in college dorms with steam heat and down-filled quilts. For Mary Virginia and everyone else stateside, the names of all the obscure towns and rivers must have seemed stubbornly foreign, as did the battle maps that eventually made it into newspapers, marking troop movements and clashes by so many insistent arrows. "Over there," is what Mary Virginia Peake called it on the day of the funeral. St. Vith, Bastogne, Auw, Malmedy, the Roer, the Meuse. *Over there.*

"Yes, ma'am," I said. My voice was suddenly catching. "It was a long way away. A long time ago."

But it wasn't a distant and dim memory for her. The faces and scenes were fresh. She was three years behind Dad at George Wythe Junior High School. She played flute in the school band. Her friend and Dad's sis Angeline was president of the Girl's Service Club. A semester behind them, a quiet girl named Barbara Ann Burriss served as an usher at the Wythe production of Booth Tarkington's play *Seventeen.* One day, Barbara Ann would star in a drama involving a young man home from the war named Bill Matthews.

Boys from Wythe would marry girls from Southampton, Downtown, and Foxhill. Children would be born to these newlyweds. When Al Knight, president of Wythe's 9th grade class, declined his homeroom teacher Margaret Lane's request to write a graduation speech, vice president Barbara Ann assumed the duty. "I was better in sports in those days," Knight said at his men's clothing store in May of 2011. "I wasn't so good at writing themes." Knight would finish high school and spend a lifetime running his upscale store. Another kid in their class, Charles Wornom, would retire from a pharmacy that bore his name.

Men would take jobs at the yards in Newport News building a Navy for a short-lived peace, then a Cold War; they'd pass down their jobs as welders, electricians, and draftsmen to their sons and daughters who would take seats at the apprentice school. They'd develop space craft and test wing designs in the wind tunnels at NACA, then NASA. They'd harvest oysters from the Chesapeake, walk beats as city cops, coach ball, teach school. All of the faces. All of the good times, war's disfiguring scars, kids growing up and up, friends growing gray and weary and old. Hadn't we just sung about what she was seeing through watery, blue eyes?

And when the strife is fierce, the warfare long
Steals on the war the distant triumph song,

And hearts are brave again, and arms are strong
Alleluia! Alleluia!

Mary Virginia and I stood together unmoved as my former Sunday school teachers with rolled up sleeves ebbed back and forth from the kitchen to the tables of disappearing food. I tried to follow her far-off gaze. I'd bet this is what she saw: her old friends were young, she wasn't frail, and Dad wasn't dead. Many of the boys, she whispered, didn't come home from the war. She was looking out the fellowship hall windows into even, afternoon light, seeing their gone-but-not-forgotten young faces, I suppose. I still held her hand—a smooth, velvet bag of bones. "The boys came home," she said, "not knowing what hit them."

Billy Boy was one of those young men.

I awakened just before the windows went dark and we plunged into the Chunnel. The re-circulating air immediately went stale. I got unwelcome whiffs of deodorized water from the recently flushed toilets at the end of the car, and of diesel, burning from a motor, armpits, socks on my neighbor stretched out on his seat across the aisle. After twenty minutes we rose into an English rain. France, Paris, the sun were swallowed up. Au revoir, old friend. Au revoir.

The guy across the aisle scoured the *London Times*. Carved across the front page were headlines about the wars in Afghanistan and Iraq. In the row in front of him, my boys slept. My eyes flitted between my offspring and the headlines. I uttered a prayer that Joseph and his brothers would never be sent to a hot spot half a world away. Is it selfish to pray one's sons and daughters be spared the machinery of war?

Like their father, my three sons have spent significant portions of childhood pretending to be at war. I didn't teach them this, as my father did not teach me. They picked it up. I came home from work one day and the living room was a city of blankets with my grandmother's colorful afghans draped over every piece of furniture.

"What happened here?" I asked.

"It's a fort," Joseph squealed, snatching my hand and whisking me under for a tour.

Is constructing blanket-forts a rite of passage for every four-year-old boy? Do all children learn on their own how to contort their hand into the shape of a revolver? They certainly didn't learn the words "bang, bang" from *Sesame Street* and *Mister Rogers' Neighborhood*. *Barney* wasn't the culprit, either.

I took some small comfort in being told that it's good for little boys to work out good versus evil through imaginative play, even by playing war. When my sons were younger their battle exploits took them and their friends into the fresh air of the neighborhood and the woods surrounding our house. In their early elementary years they were Jedi Knights or pirates. By fifth grade, war got grittier.

I answered the doorbell one Saturday to discover a friend of my younger sons—an ammo belt slung across his chest, orange-tipped rifle over his shoulder, a pistol and knife jammed in his jeans, and a cherub's smile on his proud, smudged face. I told him to check the weapons at the door and come in. Another pistol came out of his pants as did plastic handcuffs. He took off his shoes and scampered inside.

My kids never had such toy weapons, only sticks from the woods, handmade bows with homemade dowel stick arrows. They could borrow from John's formidable armory, but I've not purchased a single toy gun or grenade. For some reason, light sabers and plastic swords are another story. And, in a weak moment, I have purchased water guns, but insisted they be called "soakers." Like believing in Santa, I could go along with their war only so far. I don't believe instruments of war should be molded into cheap, plastic toys for children.

As Joseph approached and entered his teens, more often than not, their warring carried them to faraway, make-believe lands through their video games. Nowadays, Benjamin fights to stay alive in *Oblivion*.

"Eventually," Ben says, "you beat the game's main plot and you end up playing again and again."

The pretend war never ends. Video games with names like *Black Ops* and *Assassin's Creed* leave little to the imagination; sword fights and shoot-outs in those games leave mortally wounded guys writhing on the ground. Blood splatters the screen. Sparks fly. You get points for staying alive and for killing. If you die, you reload and pick up where you left off.

While plastic guns and toy weapons never made it past their anti-violence father, the video games did. Educational games that explored the alphabet morphed into *Tetris*, which morphed into shooting games. The racecars of *Mario Brothers* darting around those danger-strewn tracks became tanks on battlefields. Before long, my kids were squeezing the trigger on zombies.

"How do they die," I asked once, "since they're already dead?"

I am impatiently told "They are *un*dead." Apparently, you shoot them until their heads explode. In terms of staying away from purchasing hawkish toys, you could say, *I let my guard down.*

But "all the kids were doing it," my sons reported, and studies show that gaming increases fine motor skills, eye-hand coordination, and gets kids comfortable with computers, which will become even more ubiquitous. Somehow, flipping buttons on a controller is good for them. Further, as long as parents limited time in front of the screen and debriefed the games kids were playing, video violence did not beget violence on the playground. Feeling I had no choice, that the tide was running so strongly against me, I chose to believe that.

In *Call of Duty: Black Ops* you run around a compound hoping for "triple kills" and "headshots." An arsenal of weapons is available from cross bows to machineguns. I watch and cringe.

"This is gross," I say, feeling a little numb watching them play.

My boys can't hide their disgust with me. Their fingers dance across the buttons and joystick of their controller with amazing, nimble speed.

"Dad, it's *just a game!*"

Silly me.

But I'm not a complete alien to their warrior games. I played war as a kid, too, and so did Dad. The rifles Cousin Paul Parramore and Dad used—perhaps real .22's—were as tall as they were. I have that picture in a photo album. They're wearing cowboy hats and baby cheeks. I have another photo from some twelve years later when Paul and Dad were standing in their uniforms in front of a building called Bremo at Fork Union Military Academy. Dad wears his usual winning smile. He's got a boy-sized body and great big, adult-sized ears. Paulie, a year ahead of Dad, wrote in his yearbook, "A happy future to my cousin." That was 1941. Both faced a future in which war was no game.

I don't remember the neighborhood's version of the rules when we were kids. We may have had teams or picked armies. I don't remember if we were playing against each other or with each other, if we were each others' enemy or if the enemy was the unseen pairs of eyes somewhere out there, beyond our backyards. I suspect rules varied from day to day, depending on the crowd. But it was dangerous. And it was thrilling. Anything could happen. Any second it could end. Robbie Carpenter could come out of nowhere like he'd done on many days before popping me off with his plastic rifle, yelling, "You're dead, Matt Matthews! D-E-D. You're dead!"

Every step could be on the tail of a coiled viper. A mine could take off your leg before you heard the bang. Any wrong move could get you killed. Every step, every wiggle, every single breath could be your last.

We had seen the war in Vietnam on television. My parents didn't like me watching Walter Cronkite's version of it. Did they think I'd get warped? Have sleepless nights? I thought it was cool. Men streaming out of helicopters, keeping their heads low and their weapons ready. I had done that hundreds of times in the clearing at the center of the Crockett back yard. We didn't have rice paddies, but a ditch ran across the back of our lot. And we didn't have the body bags I had heard about on the news, but we pretended.

Cronkite on CBS or John Wayne in the Green Berets gave my buddies and me plenty of things to try out in our backyard skirmishes, such as how to carry your rifle for long hikes to the circle a block down the street, how not to spill your guts if you got captured, and how to spread out and follow the cryptic hand signals of the lead scout. Not everybody got the hand signals no matter how long we practiced them, but I did, because I was a pro. It was war and if you didn't learn, you died.

Our back yards filled with the bang, bang, bangs of sniper fire. A burst of machine guns would break the silence. Mothers would call their sons in to dinner, and they wouldn't come. It was a trick. Their mothers would call again, and finally they'd dart from the bushes for their back stoops, weaving. We'd all yell out the sounds of machine gun blasts and mortars. "You're dead," we yelled. "You're deader than dead. You lose." They'd fall, taking hits all over their dirty, young bodies. They'd writhe around and scream and die, then get up and go to dinner, sorry their mothers got them killed.

My older neighbor Billy Stewart was the best at these games. He corrected us when we did it wrong. Hanging from the ceiling in his bedroom were all sorts of plastic models of fighter planes and bombers. He spent hours building Sherman and Panzer tanks, Spitfires and Messerschmitts. He used hot spoons to melt dents into the plastic of his tanks, and hot pins made perfect bullet holes on the fuselages of his planes. These 'real-life' battle wounds were so cool.

One day I had been crawling on my belly down the ditch behind the thorny pyracantha at the edge of my back yard. It was very cold, but a soldier wasn't supposed to complain and I didn't. I had been on my belly the whole game. Silence had settled into the yard and it was getting colder, getting darker. I hadn't made much progress. It occurred to me that I might be the last guy alive. Everybody else might be inside warm kitchens eating meatloaf and getting ready for their baths.

I carefully stood, and walked in a crouch into somebody's backyard. It was inching past winter twilight into the full darkness of night. Billy Stewart was staggering in a slow circle with glazed eyes. I looked around before approaching him.

"Billy, what's wrong," I whispered.

"Shhh," he hissed. "I'm in shell shock."

I didn't know if I should help him or kill him, so I went inside. Mom was getting dinner on the table. Dad was looking over the top of the paper at the TV. I slid over the arm of his chair.

"Did you throw any grenades in the war, Dad?"

Silence.

"How many grenades did you throw in the war, Dad?"

More silence, this time with some squirming.

I know now he didn't know what to say. He didn't know how to answer or what I was able to hear. He didn't know what was right to say to a kid in the first grade. It is possible that he didn't know whether his frozen memories would ever thaw into words, and if they did, whether he would drown in them. I drilled him to remember what he wanted to forget. It was like cracking a safe. Each word he shared with me was pure gold, and I applied them immediately to my backyard war games with my neighbors. How could I know then that, for him, these war memories were live ordinance? And how could he be anything but stingy with them, especially around me, the son he wanted to protect? We were stubborn, and I wonder now if he was as disappointed in me as I was in him.

Mom called us to dinner, a table spread with steaming slow food.

It was pitch dark outside. That afternoon's battle still raged in my head. I had outlasted them all, except for Billy Stewart who might still be pacing the same circle with the daylights knocked out of him.

Dad shook the newspaper, folded it, and let it drop neatly to the floor. He popped the footstool down on his recliner and we rocked forward, unsteadily. He cleared his throat, as if, perhaps, to speak.

But I interrupted. "Did you pull the pin out with your teeth?" I was dying to know. "Huh, Dad? Huh?"

He looked at me through those serene gray-blue eyes of his. What did he see in all my pleading? He had been taught in the unlikely possibility of capture to surrender only name, rank, and serial number. He could never have imagined the psychological strain of interrogation by a six-year-old. Of course he changed the subject. "Let's eat," he said. "It sure smells good in that kitchen."

In my boys' game *Geometry Wars* your spaceship floats around the center of the screen while alien ships attack from every angle. You aim and shoot. Tracers blur in every direction, not unlike how I remember the actual war in Iraq beginning as the nation watched on television as "Shock and Awe" exploded in a sort of Hollywood blockbuster of death.

In March of 2003, members of the press holed up in Baghdad's Palestine and Al Rashid Hotels and filed reports from the rooftops. Real tracer bullets poured from the night sky. Bombs flared. It could have been a video game, except the images on our TVs were too grainy; real games have a crisper look than real war.

I opposed the 2003 war in Iraq—both in retrospect and real time, a position that strained relations with hawkish friends. I lamented that we had not measured the costs. Our goals, while ostensibly good—even noble—were either woefully unclear (to win the war on terror) or too fantastical (to bring freedom and democracy to the people of Iraq). The war would require another batch of infantry proudly saying goodbye to places like Fort Jackson just as the 106th had done in 1944. I went limp as I watched politicians rally our troops with patriotic speeches, flag waving, and Sousa marches, then punch their tickets for miles of dusty roads riddled with roadside bombs and chance encounters with teenagers who had visions of heaven and enough explosives strapped to their chests to melt cars.

Whether I liked it or not, Operation Iraqi Freedom had begun. I bleakly comforted myself that at least it wouldn't last long.

As our train sped towards London, the occupation of Iraq had not ended eight years after it began, though the drawdown had begun and was expected to conclude later in 2011. Soldiers were still ending up in body bags. Parents still gathered in small towns to welcome home the flag-draped coffins of their fallen sons and daughters.

Sadly, parents also gathered to say goodbye.

We began our trip to Europe seven minutes from our home at the Greenville Airport. At the last boarding call for the 11:22 flight to Atlanta, a soldier in army fatigues the color of dry cereal bent over to hug his mother. She refused to let go, patting and rubbing slow circles into his back, perhaps speaking into his ear, perhaps not. It was a long embrace. I couldn't tell whose will prevailed, but it was she who stepped out of the hug without fully releasing him. She held his shoulders firmly in strong hands, as much to keep him at an arm's length distance as to keep him within her reach. She was neither letting him leave nor allowing him to get closer. It was an intermediate stage of her goodbye, a sizing-you-up before I let you go. He was muscular. Thin but solid. Feminine and pretty, she was strong, too, and it was like she was lending her strength to him through the power of just her hands and the willfulness of her gaze.

Her eyes were locked onto his. She spoke. He paid rapt attention. I was too far away to hear them. I wouldn't want to eavesdrop more than I was doing now watching their farewell ritual. They knew that this may be the last moment they would see each other, and these may be their final words face to face. JAGs back at the base will make sure his last will and testament is in order before he's allowed to ship out. SOP. This may be their last embrace.

Her eyes did not fill with water as mine did watching from nearby. Her chin did not once tremble. She took a long, last look. Neither of them spoke during that moment. She let go or she released him—which, I am not certain. And he turned towards the ticket agent, taking such small steps for a man in such large shoes. He did not look back. She didn't move. His mother watched him hand his boarding pass to the agent, throw his large bag over his shoulder, and walk down the jetway. When he disappeared, she turned for the escalator.

This is how goodbyes are taken. It happened 16.1 million times in the Second World War. Nearly 75-percent of that number in the United States belonged to personnel serving abroad.[36] Hugs and passionate kisses from wives, sloppy kisses from children who didn't understand, pecks on the cheeks from younger sisters and grandparents, manly handshakes, pats on the back, banners and loud shouts, tight lips and trembling chins, murmured nicknames and lovers' shorthand, a few words but so much said. Solemn send offs at airports, rail- and bus-terminals in small towns, mothers standing by themselves like sequoias. The people of home are left behind. And someone is going very far away.

In 1942 the United States War Department began distributing a no-nonsense, pocket-sized book—*Instructions for American Servicemen in Britain 1942*—to American servicemen who were going to England to prepare for the invasion of Europe.[37] Most GIs hadn't been to England before. Because relations with Britain needed to remain strong, the pamphlet gave soldiers a head start in getting along. Soldiers read it in trains on their way to the harbors in Norfolk, Boston, or New York from which they shipped out. They read it on the ships going over. They read it when they moved into their tent camps in the English countryside where they drilled and awaited further orders.

"Don't be misled by the British tendency to be soft-spoken and polite," it said. "If they need to be, they can be plenty tough. The English language didn't spread across the oceans and over the mountains and jungles and swamps of the world because these people were panty-waists."

I'm not sure if Dad would have bothered reading a government-issued pamphlet. Abiding by its strictures, however, wouldn't have been a problem for him. Respect, for example, formed the foundation of his character. The pamphlet goes on to advise humility, a sanitized version of southern hospitality. Don't show off, respect their culture. Don't be surprised if blacks are on the same train as soldiers from the American South; for the Brits it is normal. Remember, the pamphlet read, we're allies in a war that some people want very badly for us to lose. Under the heading *Stay Out of Arguments*, it warns that American ways aren't better, but different. "The British don't know how to make a good cup of coffee. You don't know how to make a good cup of tea. It's an even swap."

I could have used a cup of tea as the train slowed and road signs for London and Dartford begin to appear. We entered the ragged edges of urban congestion. "No hard shoulders," announced one sign. Fellow passengers began pulling on sweaters and jackets. We eased by an outdoor platform at Ebbsfleet Station, our Starship Enterprise drawing smoothly to a stop. Ten minutes later we glided into St. Pancras, concluding easy and safe passage from the world's 24th largest city to its 18th.

At the station, we loaded up Oyster cards and hopped the packed Tube from Piccadilly to the Circle Line. It was rush hour. An older woman wearing a yellow raincoat and carrying both an umbrella and a shopping bag was jammed unapologetically under my right arm pit. The seats were packed, so I hung on from the bars on the ceiling that she could not have reached even if she took a running jump. In reasonable shoes planted shoulder width apart, she handled the jostling stops, starts, and manic curves by holding onto nothing but her umbrella, which was screwed into the floor like a school bus gear shift. She was as calm and nonplussed by the crowd as if she were presiding over a BINGO game. Being able to ride a subway without actually having to hold on led me to believe she might be a retired circus performer. She was probably MI6.

"How has the Chunnel to France changed things?" I asked.

"It's lovely," she chirped. Generous crows feet crowded the corners of her bright eyes. She wore a trendy yellow slicker and a fresh application of berry lipstick. She could have been fifty-five. She could have been seventy-five. "The girls and I pop over for lunch every now and then. It used to take half a day each way, what with flights and taxis. And the expense! But now it's easy. And delightful."

We chatted about the weather. It was sunny and mild until that morning when the rains began. They needed the rain, she said. Her conversational tone was as pleasant as her stance in this swaying car was steady. She inquired of my family and our trip. Because a terrorist or identity thief could have been lurking nearby, like under my other arm pit, I spoke in vague terms. I don't want the world to know I was traveling with my three sons—even though there were three blond, out of place

American juveniles within four feet who looked as foreign as I did. And the woman staring at me from the end of the car wasn't a stalker but my wife who watched me like a hawk because I pretended to know which exit to take.

"Is it always this crowded on the Tube?" I asked.

"Not usually, dear. But sometimes."

I noticed a funny line on the train PA system. A moment before we started or stopped, a recorded voice on Quaaludes said, "Make full use of the platform." I got the idea that meant to spread out on the platform. The train had lots of doors. Passengers didn't need to enter by the same one. If the armed services were ever to create another pamphlet about understanding the Brits, this deserves mention. And so would this: as the train pulled up, that same voice hypnotically warned passengers to "mind the gap." I am not the sharpest tool in the shed, but I finally got it. There's a *gap* between the platform and the train. Small children and Chihuahuas could fall through. You could lose your suitcase or a leg below the knee, so *mind* it.

At some stop along the way, my companion left with a friendly goodbye. She was a great ambassador for the United Kingdom, the Tube, and humankind. We exited a few stops later at South Kensington, having made full use of the platform and minded the gap the whole passage. The washed air smelled like flowers. I studied the map for a moment making sure we were on the wet sidewalks of Chelsea. I did a head count, and for some reason glanced around the pavement looking for our dog, who was an ocean away. This was the first tinge of homesickness, a reminder not to get too comfortable because my home and my life was somewhere else.

It was misting. But solid ground and armpits free of Londoners was a relief.

13

A Riddle of Steel and Stone

The English make as good a cup of coffee as tea. But the language barrier remained a challenge.

Germans operated our hotel. They spoke eloquent English, but their verbs were spring-loaded at the end of long, exquisite sentences. While I understood each word, I couldn't always decipher the sentence. It took a few exchanges for me to get into the beat of their linguistic groove. I worked on it.

The women at the Sainsbury's grocery next door spoke a dialect from Pakistan, I guessed. Or were they from India? Or Chicago? My checkout attendant nodded when I popped in for supplies of chocolate, cereal, milk, wine, and shaving cream. She was polite. But when she spoke, I understood only one in ten words: yoyo, discount, soybean. The woman at the ice cream truck outside a park on the Thames spoke Italian—I think—and adamantly refused to take the Scottish notes we had been given at a money exchange.

"We don't take that," she said, as if I should have known better. Scottish cash is not kosher in London? I had to pay for an ice cream cone with a credit card.

The man at the sandwich truck outside Tate Modern barked in heavily accented shouts. The velocity and volume of his words made them no more decipherable. The proprietor of the Japanese restaurant at the Bakerloo Station was hospitable, even lonely on her slow shift, but after "hello," we had to resort to pointing to the menu and nodding a lot. Every transaction in these commercial and human exchanges was made, but they were awkward. I had expected something more Shakespearean when it came to language. Since St. Pancras, I had not heard a single "whither thou goest." Not even a "jolly good."

Writing about New York City in 1949—that "riddle of steel and stone"—E.B. White noted, "The collision and the intermingling of these millions of foreign-born people representing so many races and creeds make New York a permanent exhibit of the phenomenon of one world." London is the same. It seethes and pops with a diversity of dress, race, religion, education, culture, and language. Watching BBC news, I was intrigued to learn that their beat was the world. They report news, not just headlines, from Indonesia, Vietnam, and Africa. International CNN focuses in-depth on world markets. I am not accustomed to television news that doesn't lead with some starlet's problems with rehab or breast implants. I made a mental note to watch less *Entertainment Tonight* when I returned to the States.

When we stepped off the train in the Mother country, I expected that we'd be greeted by the Mother tongue. I found myself wanting to tell every Londoner to speak up and to speak English. Of course, I recognized my hubris. Since when had I become the center of the cosmos? Back in the States, I had been warned not to propagate the Ugly American stereotype. I thought they meant while I was in Belgium and France. That advice applied also to London. This wasn't a problem, just another surprise-glimpse into a world that was much bigger than I had imagined.

At no time did I think the saying was more true: You can take the boy off the farm, but you can't take the farm out of the boy. I felt a lot like that as my ears adjusted to people who spoke to me using words I hardly could make out. I was way more yokel than cosmopolitan. I was on my Big International Trip acting all grown up, but I was just as parochial a Tidewater hick as ever. Like an astonished Gomer Pyle, all I could say was, "Golly."

It is a big world. I was thrilled to be wading around in it.

On one of our jaunts around London, we split up at the Tate Modern. Leaving the boys unsupervised in a museum of quality art within hands' reach felt like a dereliction of parental duty. I was mildly nervous that a bout of playful rough housing would knock a six million dollar picture off its hook. But I wanted to walk through these galleries alone with my wife. After I delivered the Cliff Notes on museum etiquette, the boys bolted recklessly away.

Wandering through the spacious galleries stirred butterflies in my stomach. Rachel had two things on her list: Rodin's "The Kiss" and one of Monet's many versions of his famous water lilies. Tate Modern has both. I expected nothing except the joy of exploring the clean, bright galleries, beginning with the gallery of large Rothkos. I know and generally like Rothko, celebrated for work that intersects expressionism's violence with abstraction's opacity. I tried to get lost in his dark, melting blocks of color, but they set a mood I was not in the mood to explore. That I found these canvases unintelligible, was no surprise. On other days, Rothkos have brought insight to me, if not clarity. Today, these are impenetrable, and I lacked the energy even to try to unlock them. I made a mental note: I could return to these pictures if I ever slipped into a depression and needed proof that life could get worse.

Jackson Pollack was another story. His painting "Summertime: Number 9A" completed in 1948 is a jangle of dribbled color and chaos and swirled madness. If my dad were to have stood before this large picture, he might have looked around the gallery thinking he'd been targeted for an episode of the old TV show Candid Camera. You've got to be kidding, is what he may have thought. Dad's art had to make a more literal kind of sense, and if possible be functional. He liked photo calendars. He liked pictures to go with the furniture and drapes. If pushed, Dad might say he liked Pollock's choice of yellow and blue. If really pushed, he might agree there is a nice flow to it. I'm just as certain that Dad would have admired the seamless, wood frame—nearly nineteen-feet wide. "Now," he might say, "making a frame like *that* took some work." Jackson Pollack might have liked my dad's no-nonsense assessment, and they possibly would have found a lot to talk about. But it would not have been about art.

On the plaque on the wall—where would laymen like me be without these literate, interesting notes?—physicist Richard Taylor suggests there is order in Pollock's seemingly random, energetic dribbles, especially at the finest, magnified level. My dad would say, "Yeah, right. You can talk about fractal patterns all you want. A house painter would be fired for such sloppiness."

In another gallery, Paul Delvaux's painting *Sleeping Venus* portrayed sensuous Venus reclining naked, slumbering, with her arms behind her head as if she is resigned to the man who is about to have his way with her. She's a hottie in a painterly way. It might be a very sexy moment if it weren't for the fact the man standing above the curvaceous Venus is a skeleton. Other naked—and agitated—beauties stand in the background, suggesting to the viewer that there was nothing sleepy about this scene.

I was ill prepared to translate this intriguing canvas, though I really wanted to get it. Was this about some fixation on death? My background in mythology was weak; Mr. Mitchum covered it in high school English, but nothing he covered shed light on this picture. Is this about sexual politics, aging lovers, and implications for the physiology of impotence? Was Delvaux subjected to some version of nightly television commercials as we moderns are about erectile dysfunction? Or, was this about some moral impotence, some breakdown of human intercourse, verbal and otherwise? What is the absurd skeleton mocking, denouncing? And how could Venus sleep so peacefully in such a charged moment? Had she been slipped a date rape drug? Was she dead?

I inched in closer, then I leaned slowly away, back and forth between the bright world of the Tate Modern and the strange, dark world of Delvaux. Yep. I could offer nothing but wild guesses as to what this picture meant. I reluctantly resorted to reading the plaque. Delvaux painted his Venus in Brussels in 1944 during the German occupation. Allied bombers were pulverizing the city. Wartime rationing had reduced life to near starvation. "The psychology of that moment," Delvaux said, "was very exceptional, full of drama and anguish. I wanted to express this anguish in the picture."[38]

Ah. Everything came neatly into focus. With Hitler and his henchmen in power, a lot about life might have looked ordinary and ideal, but things were catastrophically askew, which is why the naked folk off in the distance of the painting seem to be lamenting. "Wake up," they might be shouting to the transfixed Venus. Had the populace who *could* have stopped Hitler's madness fallen asleep? Was Delvaux rebuking the world for not speaking out against Hitler and fascism much sooner?

German Lutheran, Reformed, and United churches boldly spoke out in May of 1934 when 139 delegates assembled in the Gemarke Church in Barmen. The chief purpose was to discuss an affirmation written by pastors and theologians, including Martin Niemoller and Karl Barth, appealing to the churches of Germany to stand firm against any church accommodation to Hitler's National Socialism.

Barmen housed one of the Nazi's first concentration camps, Wuppertal-Barmen, later known as Kemna; from July of 1933 to January 1934, Hitler's Brown Shirts rounded up political opponents of the Third Reich, depositing them without trial and torturing them without remorse. They called it *protective custody*, and it was deemed necessary as a means to national security.

"Germanism is a gift of God," wrote Hermann Goring. "For a German the church is the fellowship of believers who are obligated to fight for a Christian Germany."[39] The so-called "German Christians" fell in line, espousing the union of Christianity, nationalism, and militarism as Christian truth. Hitler's rule was nothing less than God's will for the German people.

The Barmen Declaration, which rejected Nazi "totalitarian order of human life" and "other lords" except for Jesus, was debated by the delegates and adopted without amendment. The "Confessing Church," that part of the church opposed to the German Christians, rallied around it.[40] But it wasn't enough. The Declaration, obviously, didn't sway German Christians from falling in line with Hitler's programs. Ten years later Delvaux would frame his own declaration in Brussels, with oil and canvas.

War's pestilence covered Europe. Brits slept in bomb cellars. Food, gas, rubber, metal cans, cloth was rationed. If a family had the means, children were sent off to live with kin beyond war's reach. Young men of every nation were conscripted to march off to battle. Women worked in factories. Too few faithful of every tongue had cried out, "How long?" Jews in Nazi territory were quietly—and not so quietly—carted off, enslaved, incinerated. Everything took on a new normal. Delvaux seemed to be saying there are things that are unconscionable—like young women being haunted by skeletons—and just because heinous acts become freakishly normal to Hitler's mob doesn't mean they are normal.

This is the sort of reverie art lovers anticipate in good museums, and I was not disappointed. I wouldn't want a print of this Delvaux on my living room wall, but I did snap some photographs for my scrapbook because I didn't want to forget this intriguing canvas. After about an hour in the galleries, Rachel and I found our boys downstairs near the doors. They had been waiting 20 minutes.

"Did you guys see the Delvaux," I asked. "The one with Venus?"

They stared at me blankly.

"*Sleeping Venus?*"

They knew their mythology much better than I. But naming the picture sparked no recollection.

"The one with the *naked lady*—Venus—and the skeleton?"

"Oh yeah," Joseph remembered. "The one with the *naked lady*."

John Mark giggled.

"Yes, the *naked lady*," I repeated.

"Yeah, we saw that one," Benjamin chimed in. "She was good looking in a really non-sexy way. And we didn't understand it at all."

We decided to continue our walk, though there were plenty of metro stops and racks and racks of new bicycles for rent. I thought immediately of my daredevil youth when Evil Knievel inspired us to launch our bikes off homemade ramps. Once in elementary school, we neighborhood kids built a ramp at the low end of Robinson Park; the idea was that we'd peddle our bikes furiously from the top of the hill and hit that ramp at the bottom in a blaze of white light. None of us had the courage to actually do it.

Until Frank Henry.

I watched in awe as Frank hit the ramp at a hundred miles per hour and took off, sailing up and up. Except for his hands clamped on the handlebars, he had become detached from his bike, which hit the ground hard, but perfectly. His crotch hit the banana seat full force a nanosecond later and he coasted to a stop twenty yards away. He keeled over and curled up on the grass quietly whimpering, "Shit, shit, shit." No matter that his balls would take a decade to re-inflate, he had nailed the landing.

I resisted renting a bike, but I rubbed my palm on the row of seats as we strolled past. This long walk along and across the windy Thames took us as close to Number 10 Downing Street as the security guards would let us get. King Charles Street deposited us onto St. James Park where Rachel and the boys collapsed on the green grass. As with nearly every pause on this trip, I thought of Dad. Had he been here? Had he seen these buildings? Dad had a pass to London before shipping out to Le Havre. Did he tool around in a doubled decker bus or taste a few pints at a workingman's pub? Did he stroll this park?

Rachel and the boys were dragging and craved rest, possibly even IV fluids. They definitely didn't want to go with me into the Churchill War Rooms across the street. They'd let me go by myself and wait for me if I promised to go quickly.

I bought my ticket and set off on my speed walk through the basement rooms where Churchill and his war cabinet charted the war.

Because of the threat from German bombs, a subterranean set of top secret working rooms was established in London in 1938 to safeguard the War Cabinet and Chiefs of Staff. In the 21st century these rooms make you see that the war for London wasn't some far off affair. And, during the Blitz of 1940-41, London was ground zero. At night, the city was cloaked in black out. Curfews were enforced. While London shook and crumbled beneath dropped bombs, and people scrambled into shelters, Churchill was below ground plotting the next move. Sometimes, despite efforts to protect him, he'd bluster to the rooftop to watch the explosions, to watch his city burn.

My older friends tell me that the war effort in the United States was total. They remember recycling everything, worrying, praying for sons in combat and for daughters who were WACS and WAVES. They read the papers and hunched around their Airline and Philco radio consoles for Roosevelt's fireside chats. They helped staff three shifts at factories to keep war material on the way to the front. "Use it up, wear it out, do without" was a mantra that many knew by heart. But, after Pearl Harbor, and despite fears of a west coast invasion, the war for folk stateside was always "over there." Japanese-Americans in the camps in the west paid an unconscionable price. But while the rest of us prepared for attack, invasion, and bombs on the mainland, those attacks never came. Yes, ships were sunk on our east coast by lurking German subs, and a few shots were fired from Japanese subs on the west coast, but an army never landed. And after December 7, 1941, bombs never fell on our soil.

Not so in England. While the English Channel separated German soldiers from the fishermen at Brighton Beach, nothing but the Royal Air Force separated British citizens from Luftwaffe bombs. Despite herculean efforts by the RAF, Stukas and Heinkels obliterated a wide swath of London and other cities—demolishing buildings, fracturing water mains and pulverizing roads, houses and churches, bridges, rails, and schools. Some 40,000 Brits died. The RAF eventually won the air war, but at a cost. In a speech to the House of Commons on August 20, 1940, Churchill summed up the contribution of the RAF: "Never in the field of human conflict was so much owed by so many to so few."

The *Instructions for American Servicemen*: "Every light in England is blacked out every night and all night. Every highway signpost has come down and barrage balloons have gone up. . . The British have been bombed, night after night and month after month. Thousands of them have lost their houses, their possessions, and their families." Rationing had made all things hard to come by, the pamphlet continues, including soap. "Now it is so scarce that girls working in the factories often cannot get the grease off their hands or out of their hair."[41]

America was at war. Britain was in war.

Churchill's war rooms were the nerve-center. Clunky, old fashioned black telephones filled the map room. Every small room and cramped alcove was put into service. Secretaries typed and translators translated at small desks. Tiny bedrooms were adjacent to work rooms so that the Prime Minister's staff could pull all-nighters as needed and could sleep as able. It is close quarters and low ceilings—like being below deck on a ship. Arrows point the way for visitors to find the next exhibit. You could get lost down there.

After only twenty minutes, I'd had enough. I politely scooted around folk reading exhibits and listening intently to the audio-recorded guide devices. I wandered quickly through the maze of tables, glassed-in rooms, radios, and displays. Unlike at Versailles, I wasn't enjoying this race with my boys. I dodged exhibits. The way out always led to another room, another display, another example of how far flung, long, and wearing the war was. The human moles relegated to this underground labyrinth may have been daily reminded that they might not actually win the war. Who could imagine the desperation they felt whenever those feelings rarely were allowed to surface? Or did they surface every day? Or did they never go away? I wanted sunshine and green grass. I raced through the maze.

Maps papered the walls of the map room from floor to ceiling. Thousands of pin holes nearly obliterated oceans and hills drawn in relief. They once marked ship positions, troop movements, gun emplacements, and other machinery of war. How many lives might be lost if one of those pins were to move two inches west, or three east? The pin pricks tell the story: *The war was everywhere.* After these war rooms opened for tourists, a lot of families probably tried to find which pin-prick marked the place where their loved one stood, crouched, fought, died. Sons and daughters have sought to stand in the exact spot where Churchill had once stuck a green- or blue-headed straight pin.

Sons like me.

Though smoking isn't allowed anymore in the basement rooms, and it's been nearly seventy years since Churchill lit one of his eight daily cigars, I couldn't wait to get out for a taste of fresh air. I wanted to smell the outdoors. I wanted to see the sun. When I found my family flaked out on the grass at St. James Park, they couldn't begin to know how glad I was to see them, or how faraway I had felt after I went underground.

Standing at the gate of Westminster Abbey, we decided to skip five o'clock evensong in favor of an early dinner at the Thai restaurant near our hotel. I could almost hear the echoes of vespers, but Joseph looked bleary-eyed and very close to shut-down. *Lift up your hearts/ We life them up to the Lord/ Let us give thanks to the Lord our God.* Joseph and Benjamin were almost too tired to lift their legs, much less their hearts. I knew what they did not: lifting one's heart makes possible the lifting of everything else. But even I was too tired to argue this point. They trudged out toward the Green Line and I followed more slowly. I was hungry, too, and it didn't take long for me to catch up. Good food and a slow meal sounded like an excellent second choice. I wanted to be still. And I definitely wanted to forget WWII.

The waitress spoke little English, but she treated us like favorite cousins. She brought the manager over to translate the trickiness of ginger chicken and pad Thai with tofu at medium heat. Our waitress fawned over my boys with appetizers and drink refills. The manager asked how we were enjoying things so far. Our relaxed camaraderie must have said it all.

My father's prayer every night at dinner was the same. "Pardon our sins, O Lord, and make us truly thankful for these and all our many blessings." When the main courses came out, we held hands, and I used Dad's words to pray. So many sins. So great a need to change course, to forgive and be forgiven. But there are some brave, just people. And there are blessings, as well.

Our waitress had been joined by her other waitress friends who were about Joseph's age. They giggled together as they hovered about our table. "How you doing? More rice? More rice?"

There were no barriers in this place, no encumbrances whatsoever, least of all ones posed by language.

14

To Think Many A Man Made A Meal of It

The museums, restaurants, and tourist sites were beginning to run together. I needed some down time and got it at the home of one of Rachel's friends from high school. Linda lives with her husband Johannes and their children in Richmond, ten miles outside of London. When we planned this trip months before and an ocean away, Linda invited Rachel to come if we could fit it in. How could we not? Being in their home provided the domesticity our trip had lacked.

We sat on their back patio and ate until bursting. Besides an exquisite couscous that their kids prepared, Johannes had busied himself grilling a plethora of lamb chops, steaks, sausage, chicken breasts, and rows of multi-colored squash and peppers. Their four kids and our three are about the same age, and after they finished eating, which can take a teen as few as three minutes, they streamed in and out of the house while we couples talked. I kept nibbling. With Johannes, I also kept drinking beer. At one point Linda and Rachel were dancing and I snapped pictures and the kids reappeared to laugh. We posed for group photographs on their sun-blotched patio. Their youngest tottered on roller skates. Their oldest, a rising high school senior, was eager to ditch this obligatory visit for a date. Kids dispersed after pictures and we adults sat heavily back down for more chatting and laughing. We talked religion, politics in Europe, education, what life in Europe is like, and what the U.S. looks like from a citizen who lives on the other side of the pond. Each couple recounted how they met and married. Linda and Rachel talked about the sliver of childhood they spent together in Arizona.

The kids were alternately engrossed in a video game in the den and knocking an unsuspecting adult into a concussion by kicking a ball on the small patio. We burrowed into life, as we talked, ate, laughed. Cake made its way to the table at some point. The kids returned in force, like ants. Ice cream appeared and disappeared. Knives and spoons were licked. Plates were stacked.

Johannes and Linda expressed interest in our trip, generally, but specifically about what we had discovered by walking in Dad's WWII footsteps. The lessons were still coming into focus, I told them. I struggled with where to begin. I looked to Rachel, who couldn't read the S.O.S in my expression. I dived in: The war was everywhere and hurt everyone, I said weakly. I recounted the basic facts. Dad landed in Glasgow on the RMS Aquitania. They encamped in the midlands, possibly near Batsford Park, 30-miles northeast of Oxford University. The men in my dad's unit began their march from the English Channel to Belgium in late November. They were always hungry. They were always cold. And they were always tired, to say nothing of being afraid. The woods in which Dad fought and where he was captured felt ominous to me. I told them that being in that landscape and recalling my Dad's persistent silence about the suffering in that place had pressed on me that the truth of human depravity lies beyond words and I was sickened. And the roller coaster of violence, national arrogance, and genocide had rolled all the way into the 21st century.

Johannes and Linda's eyes grew momentarily round.

Rachel piped in. "We loved Belgium. It was so beautiful. And Paris was really fun. We went to Versailles and saw the gardens."

So, it hadn't all been darkness. And I was not a total depressive.

Linda didn't seem to mind that I had become a black hole. "It is amazing you're doing this," she said, seriously enthusiastic. "Johannes' dad was in the war and he never talks about it. We actually know very little."

I knew that Johannes' dad was in the German army. I did not know that he was a POW in a prison camp in France. Johannes somberly told the edges of the story he knew. When his father's POW camp became too full, he was moved to a working farm owned by a French family. As a prisoner, he slept in the barn and was expected to work all day, which he did. After the war, he remained friends with his former warders.

I was a bit stunned by all the food, by the friendship I felt for these strangers, and by the beauty of this breezy, sunny day. I think we were all a little amazed at how common a soldier's story is. Soldiers volunteer or are drafted. They do what they are told. No one emerges unscathed. All are called upon to do and witness grave horrors, and some do. National ideology in combat becomes slippery, giving way to the realities of staying alive. Martin King said in the woods above Bastogne, "Ask any soldier in the heat of battle who he's fighting for, and he'll tell you: 'For the man next to me.'" Some of those soldiers live beyond the war. They marry and have children. I felt shocked and grateful that two sons—Johannes and I—could share a meal outdoors on a patio on a blustery June day.

We interrupted each other with the passing of the last of the couscous and sausages and the filling of glasses, breaking into laughter, talking about international banking, college, and brands of English beer. The kick ball appeared in and out of our peripheral vision from time to time, careening around our unprotected heads. Their youngest daughter still staggered around on roller skates. And Rachel and Linda drew us along as they recalled the growing up years they spent together.

This feeling of fulfillment is how I feel when administering the sacrament of Holy Communion at my church. I break the bread and pour the cup as is the custom. I say words the congregants have heard before, words like "remembrance" and "joyful feast." I invite the church officers forward to help serve. I pray.

I feel surrounded by a cloud of all the persons whom I've ever loved. And as people in the church shuffle forward for the bread and wine, I fully expect the distant and long-dead to line up with them. People whom I still love. Jiggs Mackenzie who sang monotone with an enthusiasm to rival my dad's. Adam, a suicide, my nephew. Mr. Woolson. Charles Hunt who never let me ride his Tennessee Walkers but always had a ladle for me at his well on Mount Nebo in Arkansas. White haired and bright smiling Les Grady who would have carried me on his back if I asked. Myrtle and Bill Underwood who, in their old age, were slow, kind, and ever-steady; when they painted their house, she wore men's underwear on her head to keep paint out of her hair. Jay Brown with an off-color joke and a wink. They're all there. My childhood friends are there and they are still beautiful. Frank's not drunk. Bret's parents are coming up to the table to taste a little bread and wine, and then, after the service, will go home to the family whose hearts were ripped out when they were lost at sea in a Navy helicopter crash. And there is my dad, humming something that could be construed as a hymn as he approaches.

They are all there, everyone. They come forward. They smile. They touch my hand. I offer them the loaf of bread. They tear off some crust. Nobody has the shakes. Every teenager who froze to death in a fox hole is present and accounted for. Every child who had looked both ways and thought the road was clear approaches the table unlimping and trusting again. The dreamers, whose lives never approached their original vision show up, as do the CEOs shackled by their gold and silver handcuffs, too late to escape from jobs in which they feel trapped. The teachers who love their work and their students present themselves with contented smiles. The boy who vibrates with excited electricity because he's head over heels for the girl in line behind him. The elderly women who have been widows longer than wives. Curious children who look into the cup and are astonished to see their own reflection in the round pool of indigo liquid.

Love—God's compelling, irresistible love—has made them one. The suicide bomber and the US Marine. The husband who can't remember his wife of sixty years. The blue and the gray. The black and the white. The yellow and the red. The criminal and his victim. They come without a trace of shame or malice. The estranged don't feel out of place, nor do the unranked, the unlanded, or the undone. No one is turned away. It is a convention of loved fools who—miracle of miracles—are for one snowflake of transcendence completely right with God. *Taste and see that the Lord is good,* says the Psalmist. And what a taste it is.

The shade from the tarp over our friends' patio had lengthened to cover me. I went to put on my sweatshirt but it was still wet. A sudden shower had caught us on our walk from the bus. Johannes retreated inside and brought me a thick striped sweater. He had given it to his father as a gift, but his father gave it back to him after a year because he had grown frailer and the sweater seemed to keep getting bigger. I put it on. It was a perfect fit. I'd return it before we left. I felt warmed by more than cotton blend.

After a really good meal among friends, Dad would often say, "To think that many a man made a meal of it." It was an off-handed compliment to the cook, usually my mother. It was also an off-handed prayer of thanks.

On the first anniversary of my dad's death, Mom and I illegally dumped his ashes into the harbor from the seawall behind a house on Chesapeake Avenue. At the graveyard near Langley Field, several of my family are buried, and Mom and Dad's marker is in their midst.

Years later, after moving out of town, I was in Hampton, and I spent an afternoon trying to find the marker. When I go to funerals—and my profession requires that I go to many—I am adept at following the temporary signs to where the graveside service will be held. A pile of dirt covered with a square of plastic grass, a small tent, and some folding chairs are usually the giveaway. After the funeral, however, all of the headstones or markers look the same and the graveyard roads tangle in a spaghetti-web of twisting circles. You need a great memory or a map to find your way.

At the office for the graveyard—euphemistically called a *memorial park*—the receptionist was efficient and pleasant. She picked up a phone, asking for coordinates for Dad's grave. She invited me to sit. Nobody has bigger portraits of themselves than founders of funeral homes. And no Muzak is more nauseating than religious Muzak. But funeral home stuffed chairs are always among the most comfortable of any waiting room seats and the candy dishes are always full of wrapped mints. Grieving people need all the comfort they can get in their sorrow, hence soft chairs and high-class mints. When a funeral director emerged from the back, she informed me that my dad wasn't at this *memorial park*. I told her his marker surely was here, right next to the grave of my uncle, for whom I performed the graveside service. I checked her spelling. I made sure Dad's name didn't have a suffix. I looked out the front window to make sure I was at the right graveyard. "I'm nearly positive I'm at the right place. Can you check again?" She returned to the back.

When the director reemerged, her smile made me know all was well. Yes, Dad's marker is, indeed, in this *memorial park*. But his file was still mistakenly in the living file, not the deceased file, which threw her. Dad was in the living file, not the dead file. Not a bad illustration for a sermon one day, I thought. His plot was number 107. He was in the Jesus the Good Shepherd Garden. She gave me a map. A deep longing crept upon me as I went out to find the site.

I found the marker even though the map looked like something M. C. Escher might draw. I think I had seen the bronze marker only once—soon after Dad died. I found Mom's, too. I can't imagine spreading her ashes in the bay, but I will if she insists. A flower garden would be a more likely place. Hers might actually get buried. Regardless, I'll make sure her name ends up in the proper file at the graveyard office. I'll also make sure her death dates—the only thing missing from her marker—are properly installed. I don't look forward to that day.

Mom's parents were there. Her soft spoken dad—my Deda—was sixty-seven when he died of complications from the heart attack he suffered at the men's lunch at church listening to Dr. Ben Lacy Rose, a beloved Union Seminary professor. Mom's brother—the uncle I idolized—was only forty-nine. He died a dozen years after his father. Bob's own mother—my Baba—cut him off in the last months of his life when he came out to her that he was gay. He was dying of cancer and perhaps wanted her to know the deeper truth of his relationship with his partner of two decades. Maybe he didn't want her to find out after he died, so telling her was intended to be a kindness. I think he wanted her to accept the real him, not the man she imagined, the son she bragged about but had pegged all wrong. Sadly, she would not. The news broke her. She howled and beat her basement walls and wrote letters to California begging him, literally, to repent lest he go straight to hell. It was the only way she knew how to love him. I hope his love for her was bigger than hers for him, even great enough to understand. And now Deda, Baba, and their only son Bob are buried side by side. Jesus the Good Shepherd, clutching a lone sheep in his concrete arms, stands above them smiling kindly.

Others of my family are there. And I began to miss them terribly.

Dad's oldest sister Mary Louise who died young—at fifty—prompted the family to purchase a group of plots here. I was a child when she died and even when I look at pictures of her I remember nothing about her. The pictures capture an infectious smile, and her siblings often spoke of her, after her death, as if she were very much alive, only living in Montana or Greece. Her untimely death stunned everyone. A massive heart attack felled her in the teacher's lounge one morning at Thorpe Junior High School where she taught. Her last words were, "I have a terrible headache."

I called my cousin Dave on my cell phone, asking him to guess where I was standing at that very moment. He was in a thunderstorm at a gas station in Alexandria dreading rush hour on traffic-clogged, slick roads. "Where?" he asked over the din of hail pounding his roof. I was suddenly too emotional to speak. The tips of both shoes were touching his mom's, my Aunt Angeline's, name.

I looked again at Dad's marker before heading to my car. The words on it took me aback.

SGT US ARMY

WORLD WAR II

Free grave markers from the Veterans Administration require branch of service to be listed. Dad wasn't cheap, but you can't argue with free. When he and Mom prearranged their funeral plans, he must have agreed that a government marker would be applied for. Upon his death, 40-1330 or its predecessor VA Form authorizing Dad's grave marker was among the sheath of papers Mom had to fill out and sign.

He spent his whole life trying to forget, but that damned war followed Dad all the way to the grave.

15

Bridge Over Troubled Water

I had to get to the Clyde River. I was running out of time. There was still something for me to discover that I hadn't found yet, but I felt that whatever it was was still within reach. I didn't know what eluded me, but trusted that I'd recognize it when I saw it. That's why, even though I was becoming wearied from this great journey, I was eager to set out for an overnight jaunt to Edinburgh and Glasgow. The Aquitania, the ship that hauled over my dad and 10,000 other GIs from NYC, probably anchored off Greenock (maybe Port Glasgow), which served as the main assembly point for convoys of transport ships plying back and forth across the Atlantic. I wanted to hear gulls, feel moving water beneath a humming deck, see the land from the vantage of the water. There I hoped I would find a clue, receive a sign. I had to get on that river.

Not a small part of the Second World War was getting there, and the RMS Aquitania was no tinny boat. A jewel of the Cunard Line, she steamed half a million miles during the war, hauling nearly 400,000 passengers around the globe.[42] For Dad, who had hardly traveled outside Virginia before he joined the army, walking up the gangplank onto this mighty ship amongst the rank upon rank of fellow soldiers must have twisted his gut with terror and flooded his body with enough adrenaline that he tingled with excitement.

At 24-knots, she ranked among the fastest ships on the seas. Armed escorts could not keep up, so she sailed alone. But the passage was anything but quick or smooth. GIs like Robert Towle[43] were told the Aquitania changed course every 19 minutes because it took 20 minutes for a German sub to complete the complicated process of aiming and firing a torpedo. Whether such intricacies of U-boat targeting were true or not, the Aquitania zig-zagged across the ocean. Men below decks heard the constant rattle of the rudder chains, the strained thrum of engines pegged at full steam. Men above, avoiding the *barfatorium* in the tight quarters below, hung over the rail "looking for periscopes" and swearing never again to touch booze; they saw miles and miles of Zs churned white by four 16-foot propellers as their luxury liner carried them farther and farther from home. They departed Manhattan's pier 84 around Halloween, 1944. What should have taken five days in a straight line took seven days along a very crooked route instead.

The Army manned guns mounted fore and aft just in case a German sub appeared. Wade L. Anderson from Hico, Texas, was part of a four-man crew on a 40mm in her bow. That and the 20mm and 3-inch guns must have been for show, because if a torpedo were launched, guns would have done no good. One lucky German strike wouldn't give most of the men on any of the nine below decks time to scurry topside. Aquitania would have become a 902-foot steel coffin. If these men had paid attention in their high school history class, they would have remembered pictures of the torpedoed Lusitania sinking like a plumber's wrench in 1915. It took only 18-minutes for that beauty to slip forever beneath the waves of the North Atlantic.

Anderson worked at his post four hours on, eight hours off, around the clock for two years. Another gunner, Jimmie Moler, made 37 crossings from New York to Scotland: seven days over with new troops, seven days shore leave, then seven days back with the wounded.[44]

Having grown up on the bay and been gifted with sea legs, Dad didn't find the seas sickening as did many others. He explored. It took only moments to discover that the Aquitania was more than a troop transport. Dad had never been near Georgian lounges, regal bars, and such a collection of master workmanship, exotic woods, and ironwork. Once the "Gracious Lady of the Sea" offering 33-day South American cruises, Aquitania was now a transit bus skidding back and forth across the Atlantic. She—like my father and *all* the men crammed aboard—was created for better things than a shabby passage like this.

Aquitania's bow rode higher than her stern as though she was built to show off. She had not only muscle but *swag*. In better days, she gleamed; her black hull and four stacks rose magisterially above a bright red water line. Artists fondly painted her in harbor with nearby tugs smaller than they actually were. Landlubbers wouldn't notice but enthusiasts would understand. Aquitania was bigger than life.

Growing up in a family of five on his dad's army salary during the depression, Dad was unaccustomed to luxury. The three-bedroom home on Cherokee Road in Hampton was ample enough for his four siblings and the neighborhood dog they sometimes kept, but it was no mansion. "They had one of everything," Aunt Alice remembers, "and it all had belonged to [older brother] Jimmy." Few if any of Dad's neighbors could have afforded a prewar cruise on the Aquitania.

By the time Dad's 422nd boarded, Aquitania's clean whites and reds had long been glopped over with wartime gray. Even though Irene Manning's small USO show was meant to perk up the troops—and the WAVES and WACS also making the passage—it was a glum ship on a gloomy mission. Originally designed to *transcend* as much as transport, a fully booked passage consisted of just over 4,000 people, including over 800 crew and 660 pampered souls in first class. At the outbreak of WWII, Aquitania was refitted to carry nearly ten thousand troops. Hanging canvas bunks transformed staterooms into crude dormitories. So much for dancing in the ballroom or strolling the promenade. A full load of guys weighed down with gear they could barely carry were sacked out everywhere. Joseph F. Littell, a Bulge veteran, wrote that the 106th was the "youngest, greenest bunch of peach-fuzzed" men ever to set sail. "Most of us, no more than eighteen or nineteen years old, had been taken almost in mid-milkshake from the corner drugstore."[45]

For those who dared to eat, nearly 500 men stood at counters shoveling in dehydrated eggs, bully beef, and stale rolls. Another 500 hungry men impatiently waited their turn. Linen and fine dining had been reduced to chow lines. In a ship that once served roast pork, stuffing, and ox tongue, Private Kenneth Grant remembered that "Some men preferred to live on Hershey bars and cookies from the canteen. For those brave enough, the showers employed cold salt water."[46]

Dad played a lot of craps and poker on the passage over. GIs gambled with English money that very few knew how to count. Towle writes that it felt like playing with coupons or bus tokens. A pound was worth a buck to them, Towle writes. "Some of those pots that were full of 'bet a buck' coupons would pay an Englishman's salary for a month. We didn't know or care because we always had a few American dollars in our pocket as this stuff looked like play money." Dad's disposition was *sunny* before the war, his sister said, and this bright demeanor translated well in poker. He never let on he had a bad hand or a good one. He was relaxed, didn't finger his cards, always smiled. He bluffed his way to a few jackpots, turning his winnings into a bribe that got him a bunk in the kitchen and all the hot food he wanted—without the lines.

Being shoehorned into what had formerly been one of the most luxurious liners in the world was at best a foreboding passage into the frightening machinery of a once-distant war getting closer with every turn of the screw. As the RMS Aquitania pitched uneasily towards Glasgow, surely something inside of these anxious men rolled and zigged and zagged.

I bristled with excitement as our train to Edinburgh jostled us north. This trip's rainbow end plunged beneath the waves of the Clyde in Glasgow and soon I'd be there. Mostly it was the greens I feasted upon out the generous windows as we surged beneath partly cloudy skies and over hilly terrain. In a rare display of color, red poppies stood at attention like new recruits near Wetherby. White flowers filled the ditches parallel to the tracks, then, beyond, poppy-red oozed like rivulets of lava.

I dozed, fidgeted, listened to music, pretended to read. Gulls gave the first clue that we were nearing the coast. Fields disappeared over cliffs above the North Sea. The towns of Alnmouth and Berwich-upon-Tweed, to name just two, nearly astonished me.

I leaned over to Rachel and pointed to the town on the coast, below the track. "I want to move there."

"When," she asked.

"Right now."

Rupert Brooke, who died of sepsis from a mosquito bite in WWI, wrote about the English soldier in the trenches pining away with thoughts of "breathing English air, Washed by the rivers, blest by suns of home." It would be easy for a lonely soldier to long for these pastoral scenes.

I wondered what Dad missed when the Aquitania bore him to war. What did he dream about?

The smell of the bay, for sure, is something Dad missed. At low tide, the muddy creeks stink of rotting seaweed. He missed that because it meant crabbing. When the wind blew from the right direction, you could smell the steamed crabmeat being picked from the dock sheds founded a hundred years ago by a cousin named McMenamin.

Army Air Force Pfc. Rae Marlin Litaker—like many GIs—missed everything about his North Carolina home. In his unpublished letters to his mother—discovered in July of 2011 in a sewing box at the estate of his late sister—Rae asked his "Mother dear" to share these words with his whole family. "You are wonderful—all of you. I suppose it took a war to make lots of boys realize what families, friends, and home is. Now I know, as I have never known before."[47]

At the reception after Dad's funeral, as we milled around the fellowship hall eating and visiting, I came upon an unfamiliar elderly man. He had just stuffed half a pimento cheese sandwich into his mouth and was busy chewing. I shook his hand. "Thanks for coming," I said. He nodded looking a little embarrassed, unable to utter a word from his mouth oozing the glue of cheese and bread. I searched his face trying to place him. I couldn't, though he certainly knew me. Jaws still working, he pointed to me, then lowered his palm in slow motion towards the floor to an imaginary line below his waist. He winked. He either wanted me to sit, or was saying, *I knew you when you were this tall.*

It's nice to be known by people you don't know. Older people in the neighborhood whom Dad did not know missed him when he was away at war. They missed him, and prayed for him, and asked about him. They looked forward to the day when all sons and daughters were home safe. They hoped that young men and women could resume their lives. They longed for a future that they knew for many would not come. They wanted for Dad to have his chance.

When the adventure of travel wears off and the gung-ho of war songs is shattered by melting steel and weakening shrieks, everything about home takes on romantic overtones. Anywhere is better than here. While Dad would never have said it as Rupert Everett did, he would have wholeheartedly agreed. Dad, also, longed to be blest by the suns of home.

Getting closer to Edinburgh, we passed the bridges festooned with the requisite graffiti you'd expect at the gates of a major city. "I love figs" stood out. Besides graffiti, I noticed what people were wearing on the outdoor platforms we stopped at on our way into the city. A few folk wore short pants, but most of them had woolen sweaters on— real, winter sweaters. Women wore long coats and trendy but warm scarves. With each stop closer to Edinburgh, colder air whooshed into the train car with the new passengers.

"We're going to have to buy serious jackets," Rachel said.

Another unbudgeted expense, I thought. I felt foolish because I didn't even pack a jacket. I thought about it, but on the day I stuffed my clothes in a suitcase in South Carolina it was 97-degrees. I packed underwear, a *New Yorker*, socks, short pants, ink pens, headphones, an extra toothbrush, baby powder, a deck of cards, one necktie, and a few more BVDs. A bulky jacket would just take up space. It was just one more useless thing to keep up with that I wouldn't possibly need, I remembered muttering to myself.

At the Waverly station in Edinburgh, I spied a man in shorts. *There!* I comforted myself. *I'll be fine in my jeans and my lightweight sweatshirt.* Besides short pants, he wore a down-filled ski vest. And it was zipped up to his chin.

A f t e r c h e c k i n g i n t o a n *economy* h o t e l, our first destination was a six o'clock concert at St. Giles Cathedral. We had traveled too far not to spend some time in our distant mother church. Friends and church members at St. Giles Presbyterian Church in Greenville, South Carolina, would expect no less.

Matthew McAllister and Aisling Agnew charmed us with chamber music for guitar and flute. Many teens would have hemorrhaged with boredom. Mine were bored, too, but musically curious. I was glad. That stone sanctuary could make any music better with ceilings reaching for the stars and stained glass windows that capture and bend starlight into images of saints, water, and flame.

My boys and I share musical interests and tastes. I introduced them to my musical library of such disparate sounds as Electric Light Orchestra and Simon and Garfunkel. They like Yes and the Beatles, the Stones and Nickel Creek, Frank Sinatra and Joe Satriani. They've introduced me to their tunes. I like the Killers, and Fun, and Mumford and Sons. And thank goodness they introduced me to The Barenaked Ladies, who have inched into the top five of my favorite bands. We've been to Broadway musicals together, coffee houses, and local gigs featuring local musician-friends and old timers on their nostalgia tours. We've discovered music together.

Music was more a collision between me and Dad than the connection I so enjoy with my own kids. I'd turn up Supertramp or Jimmy Buffet on my bedroom stereo and he'd holler, "Turn it down!"

He'd listen to the Metropolitan Opera—with the volume on low—when he worked out in the garage on Saturdays, which, to me, sounded as discordant as grinders and table saws. As I got older, and as I paid more attention, I realized he liked American Songbook in general, but Big Band in particular.

He didn't like rock and roll, which was the soundtrack of my teenaged life. The ubiquitous pop band ABBA, bordering close to the disco that my peers and I were supposed to hate, summed up the message I wanted to tell every pretty girl in my school: "Take a chance on me." I wished Dad had once asked, "What does that song mean to you?" Though he wasn't a man of many words, even he might have had the insight to suggest one of those pretty girls might take a chance on me if I first took a chance on her. Just because he wasn't a talker didn't mean he didn't have anything to say.

Besides standing shoulder to shoulder in church singing hymns, Dad and I didn't share music with each other. There is one notable exception: outdoor band concerts at Fort Monroe. Each Thursday night of the summer, the United States Continental Army Band gave a free concert to anyone who wanted to spread a blanket, sit on the grass, and listen. Mom usually packed a terrific picnic, as several hundred other folk did, and, as we'd eat pasta salad and ham biscuits, the band rocked through classical, big band, and Sousa marches.

People sat on the steps of the grand old Chamberlain Hotel. Lovers held one another on the sea wall by the harbor as ships and tugs scudded out into the darkening bay. At the back of the bandstand, which sits near the center of the big field, scores of children played; they tossed frisbees, blew bubbles through soapy wands, batted balls back and forth with field hockey sticks, spun cartwheels, kicked soccer balls, threw foam footballs, and generally ran around having a blast. Busloads of senior citizens perched on lawn chairs sharing cheese and summer grapes; some folk in wheel chairs enjoyed being pushed along the wide sea wall, wind in their hair, free. Boy Scouts sold hot dogs.

People came from all over Hampton and beyond. It was a great celebration of summer, of music, and of community.

When I was a kid, I'd bump into friends I knew. After college, I'd enjoy bumping into their parents.

When my kids were born and before their Pops died, we'd often head over to the bandstand at Fort Monroe. On one evening when Joseph was six, he and I were lying on our backs marveling at the moving shapes the clouds made. On our imaginary flying carpet arrayed in the school colors of my wife Rachel's Texas college, we were a million miles away from terra firma and all we could see was sky, until a little stranger-girl wandered onto our blanket and leaned into our field of vision. Her little one-and-a-half-year-old head was framed by blond curls. She laughed, and Joseph and I rolled over to see her father standing behind Rachel at the edge of our gaggle. His eyes seemed to ask whether or not his little daughter was interrupting us. And something about our look back must have indicated that she wasn't. She plopped herself down on my chest and let me bench press her up and down above my head into the migrating clouds. Then, she wandered off on stumpy legs across the sidewalk into another cluster of folk, and her amiable dad strolled along behind. Those Thursday nights at the band concert were full of surprises.

My dad didn't like my bands. Not Journey. Not even Rush. But he and Mom took me to the band concerts at Fort Monroe. And I'll never, ever forget those humid summer evenings. A harvest moon glowed brighter and brighter as the hot pink sun dropped lower and lower, finally vanishing like a coin in a candy machine below Newport News Point. It was a Hollywood ending to a hot August day. The wind was stiff from the bay, damp and salty and cool. Everyone was sharing—food, blankets, conversation, *and music*. Squeezed between an Aaron Copeland medley, "The Chattanooga Choo Choo," and "Mack the Knife" was the sound of horns from tug boats and applause from the appreciative crowd. I remember running around catching fireflies.

We left St. Giles Cathedral humming catches of the sonatas we had just heard. Walking quickly in a scrum to stay warm, motivated by cold and hunger and one of those recurring and sudden needs to be close, we headed for a restaurant we had seen near the hotel. The boys were loudly getting up the nerve to order haggis for dinner.

"Aw," Rachel said. "It's not so bad."

"Yeah," Benjamin said, "if you don't mind eating LUNGS!"

"It's like sausage," Rachel argued.

"Ew!" We all groaned, even Rachel.

We sped along Rose Street past the Assembly Rooms to a place called The Filling Station. They had a warm booth for five in the back.

16

If Only I'd listened to Sherlock Holmes

We gobbled boxed breakfasts in our rooms then loaded up for the hike back to Waverly Station. Rachel and I sat across from one another on the 9:12 commuter to Glasgow. The countryside soaked up the warm slants of morning sun. Our boys huddled across the aisle guarding secrets in their tight circle. The grey haired architect sitting next to Rachel busied himself with the Scottish edition of the *Daily Telegraph*, but not before answering my barrage of questions. He grew up in Brighton. He thought the architecture in Glasgow isn't as appreciated as it should be. And, during his adolescence, he devoured Thin Lizzy music.

As the train rocked slowly west, I studied Rachel's face. She squinted in the strong light. She's worn glasses since she was seven. The lenses magnify and brighten her blue eyes. Her short blonde hair will lighten to white soon. Her smile will always bring me calm.

Her knapsack was at her feet. She kept checking it until we were well underway. She didn't notice that I was watching her take inventory. She patted her pockets, and fingered her watch and earrings. When our eyes met, she gave me one of those married people glances that I correctly took to mean, "Where are our children?" These three young men hardly need shepherding anymore, but I indicated all was well with a nod. Our ideas of child welfare have always differed, so she twisted around to see for herself. Yes, they were there, all three, situated, okay. She settled, contenting herself, finally, to looking out the window. We are forever seeing things from different perspectives. Because of our opposite seating, she watched what we were leaving behind and I watched where we were going. Except for train rides, usually it's the other way around. I'm the one who spends a lot of time looking back.

We have been married nearly twenty-five years. When we met she used the word *marvelous* a lot. She was curious about life. She and her friends at the seminary were known to take afternoon tea. She busied herself with theological studies and arranging monthly dinners for our international classmates. I played community volleyball on long afternoons before dinner in Lingle Hall, and I busied myself mightily with dating her, this diminutive blonde from Texas who gave me a *look* that made me feel like one of God's favorites. I wouldn't have chosen the word *marvelous* to describe the feeling, but that fairly summed it up.

We were as old now as some of the *old* people we knew in Richmond at Union Seminary. Both of us approaching fifty, I wanted to think we were aging with grace. Rachel is.

When my father was my age he had had his first heart attack. His doctor said it was a wake up call to stop smoking and give up fried eggs for breakfast. He did both for a season, but Mom hardly knew how to cook without sugar and eggs and bacon grease, and Dad didn't know what to do with his hands. The heart attack also reminded him, possibly for the first time since the war, that he wouldn't live forever.

When he died, Rachel said it was like he just got off the train and we kept right on going. We were going still, on the 9:12 to Glasgow. And, amazing to me when I stopped to take account, we had been going without him for nearly a decade.

Sixty minutes flew by. The architect folded his paper and wished us well. We wandered into the station, found our legs and the restrooms. We stepped outside, but were not sure where the river was. My family was looking to me for direction, and I supposed I was looking bewildered, because an elderly man in a Scots Rail uniform asked if he could help. I told him I wanted to get to the Clyde River. He must not have got asked that question every day because he paused. He looked concerned. I told him I was following my dad's WWII footsteps. I told him about how Dad arrived in Scotland on the RMS Aquitania when he was a GI in WWII.

His eyes lit up.

"*Aquitania.*" He repeated the ship's name in a far off voice like it had mystical powers. "My sisters and I sailed on the Aquitania to Canada in 1941 to go live with an aunt. Our parents wanted us out of the war," he said. "I remember her well."

I tried to imagine him as a child. Thick, red hair, ruddy cheeks, pale skin. He was portly now, hair turned white but still thick and wavy. He had a boyish spirit despite a body shrimping from wear and a skin splotched with age. Drooping jowls swayed when he moved. He wore a warm grin. The Aquitania had a power over this kindly man that the Clyde River seemed to have over me.

"What do you want to see on the Clyde," he asked excitedly.

I dared not confess that I yearned to feel the power that the river alone could convey through a hull and deck to my feet. I needed to feel the water on which my father was borne onto this warring continent. "I just need to see the river," I said awkwardly.

We were standing close together. The old man didn't speak but looked into my eyes. He must have been eighty. Why was he still working, I wondered. Was he a volunteer? Did his pension not work out and he still needed an income? Did he love the trains? Did a wife back home want him out of the house a few hours each day? If I had thirty minutes with him—even twenty—I'd have an answer to those questions. I am my father's son. I can chat a guy up pretty well, too.

"I fully understand," he said after a silence that was meant, I supposed, to convey respect. I actually thought he *might* understand. He clapped one hand on my shoulder, gave it a squeeze, and pulled me near, not unlike Martin did on that battlefield ridge; with the other hand, he pointed us down the street and gave witheringly thorough directions. Freckles covered his sausage fingers. His hand quivered. Maybe he could tell that I only caught half the street names he mentioned, because he stopped mid-sentence. He pointed emphatically. "That way," he said. "You can't miss it." His eyes were glassy and blue.

"Good luck," he said, shaking my hand again.

He was right. You can't miss the river. At the place where we accessed it, drab, low-rise buildings dressed in concrete, steel, and glass crowded up to Broomielaw Road. This block certainly is not one of the architecturally noteworthy ones our morning train companion had in mind. Several steps down from the patched asphalt street spread the wide concrete walk that parallels the gray water troubled by a cool wind and strong currents. Concrete seawalls on both sides hem in and tame the forlorn Clyde; she reminded me of some Pharaoh's cat locked in a cage at the pound.

I've never seen a river content in its banks. The seawall along the Boulevard back home does little to contain the James when rains come and a nor'easter blows the green waters black. The Clyde could swell above these walls as easily as the Western Branch did when Rachel and I lived in Portsmouth; as Hurricane Isabel bore down, our neighbors on the water side of the street who stayed home moved their cars up the block to higher ground. The water kept coming. Wading through knee-deep water to the road, husbands eventually carried their wives out on their backs.

When I was a kid living on Maynard Street, Dad and I once packed the family silver in the trunk of the Impala when the edges of a bad storm whipped the harbor into froth. Mom had gone to church. Dad and I stayed home and watched the water creep into the garage before it finally stopped. The Clyde could snap her tail and fill every basement in Glasgow.

"Eventually, all things merge into one," wrote Norman Maclean, "and a river runs through it." Maclean was haunted by waters. Maybe I am too. I was certainly haunted by the Clyde, and as my thoughts turned to the water, they became kaleidoscopic, tossed and jumbled as by waves.

Dad taught me to revere the water. Some body of water touched his life at every important juncture. When he was a child, Dad learned to row on the flat waters of Indian River Creek. Ihren Creek in the Belgian woods quietly received the pieces of Dad's dismantled rifle and of the photograph of his father moments before surrender. After liberation he no doubt watched lovers stroll along the Seine. He swam, crabbed, and clammed in the Hampton Roads along Chesapeake Avenue; and on the other side of that harbor, only four miles away, Los Angeles class subs and aircraft carriers lined the terminals at the Norfolk Naval Base. The blinking lights of that horizon look like Christmas every night, crowning such brute force and nuclear strength with festive dots of colored light. All that water, those rivers and streams and bays—along with the proud, Scottish Clyde—flow unstoppable to the sea. And they each lifted my father, anointed him along his life's way.

We grabbed a quick lunch at a cafeteria, then took our place at the ferry gate on the seawall. We were first in line.

After 45-minutes of standing around, getting antsy, I wondered what was wrong. We craned our heads peering up and down the river. The river was bereft of traffic—no barges, no tugs, no pleasure craft, and definitely, no ferries. Another couple waiting near us also leaned against the rail at river's edge waiting; they might have been father and daughter. They didn't need this ride in the way that I did.

I finally called the phone number on the gate that led to the gangplank.

The woman who informed me that the ferry was out of service could not have been nicer. I could not contain my disappointment. Pacing up and down the seawall, I told her that I had come all the way from the United States of America to ride on that ferry.

She may have wanted to say that I needed to get a life, but "Sorry" is all she did say, and she said it in a small but professional voice.

"Are there other ferries?"

"No," she said, sympathetically.

I wanted to hate her, but it was difficult to do so. She had done no wrong.

"The normal schedule will resume on Tuesday."

"But not today? Not later this afternoon?"

"No."

"Not this evening?"

"Not today," she soothed.

I was mad at myself for not booking something in advance. I'm a planner. I'm not great at being spontaneous, and this slight catastrophe was one reason why. There was nothing else for either of us to say. After a long pause I thanked her.

"You're welcome," she said. "There's absolutely nothing I can do."

There is absolutely nothing I could do, either. Nothing. I felt helpless.

I broke the news to my family. They sloughed it off.

"Let's go back downtown and buy t-shirts," Benjamin said, bouncing on the balls of his feet. My bright-eyed boy was eager to put more movement into the day.

"I want a kilt," Joseph said.

They were aware I was upset. I had not shared my hopes of the Clyde with Rachel, but she understood a little bit, I think, so she said she'd walk the boys back to the inviting shopping plaza on Buchanan. I told them I'd catch up in a few minutes. They headed off, not sure what they missed, not sure what I wanted.

Standing alone by the pedestrian bridge over the river, looking upstream and down, I had stumbled upon a truth: being stuck on this seawall, not in control, had delivered me to my dad's side 68 years before. Dad and all those other GIs had felt helpless, too. Beyond being expected to win the war, they knew nothing of the big picture and their role in it. They just followed orders. GIs didn't make plans. They knew what it was like to be stuck waiting. They knew what it was like to be kept in the dark, on the sidelines as the river swept past.

Another thought emerged from river's edge. I had been trying to wish it away since Normandy, but it had haunted me. I couldn't climb aboard that ferry any more than I could step into my dad's army-issue boots. I could motor the 20-plus-miles to Greenock near the Firth of that ancient river, but I would not have found my dad on those waves. I could rub my fingers through the steel dust at the Brown Shipyard from which the Aquitania rose one majestic deck at a time but I would not have understood his war experience significantly better. I could ride all the way to the top of the cantilever Finnieston Crane at Clydebank overlooking the shipyard. In her day, she could hoist 150-tons, but she is powerless to lift the mystery that shrouds the war experience that Dad could not, would not share. He didn't talk about his training, the battle, his capture, what he saw, or what he wished he never saw.

That sliver of months in the Army—only twenty-three total—had taken him so far and shown him so much. How could he have held it all so closely to his chest? How could he have shared so little of that chapter of his life? Maybe he was invisibly damaged, crippled by survivor's guilt, ashamed his overrun regiment surrendered. Maybe he was underwhelmed with what he thought was his small contribution.

When I was grown, one of the ways Dad said goodbye was cheerily telling me to "keep it on the road" or to "keep it between the ditches." I think that's what he tried to do when he returned home. Other survivors would write about what happened *over there*, or talk it through by staying in touch with war buddies, or let it cripple them. Dad refused. He'd fought the war once, and once was enough. While it never showed on the outside, I think it took a lot for him to keep it on the road. The ditches to either side were dark and deep.

Other WWII vets talked about their part of the war and wrote books, went to American Legion meetings, spoke at Memorial Day parades, and gathered at annual service reunions. The reason we know so much about the Greatest Generation is because, eventually, *some* of the silent ones opened up.

A year before he died, while we were standing in their kitchen, Dad asked me, "What do you want to know?" I couldn't answer that question because I wanted to know everything. And I didn't know where to begin in the asking anymore than he knew where to begin in the telling. On this matter, we failed each other.

Anything I ever understand about my dad's war experience will be seen at a slant, as if looking through an antique bottle of bubbled, green glass; any image I ever hope to catch will be distorted and colored. And I am not the only one with such a circus-mirror view.

Less than five months after the end of the war in Europe, Lt. Col. Joseph C. Matthews, former Executive Officer of the 422nd and no relation to my dad, tried to make sense of what happened to the men with whom he served. He prepared a ten-point memo to his former troops. In it, he gave a 488-word summary of combat operations from arrival to the battlefront on December 10th to their final capture on the 21st. (Dad was captured on the 19th.) In 174 words, describing events after capture, he wrote about the prison camps. Ridiculously, he went on to describe the conditions under which promotions (ie: War Department Circular No. 185) and personal and unit decorations (as well as additional pay) would be awarded. These things were important to the survivors. Extra pay is a good thing, and getting rank matters, especially to those who would reenlist and make the army a career. But it seems cheap to talk about it so matter of factly, so coldly. Words failed Lt. Col. Matthews as they failed Sgt. Matthews. It was exactly that way. *Only worse.* In his ninth point he noted, "It is estimated that the 422nd Inf sustained casualties of approximately 100 killed and 750 wounded, including deaths and injuries sustained after capture." He included a partial list of the dead: Kent, Luck, Jones, Rizzoli, Rogosienski, Cohen, Lubke, Rosen, Burns, Carraturo. Those barren ten points captured the horror of those days better than a thesaurus of adjectives.

Matthews included a letter from Col. George L. Descheneaux, Jr., commander of the 422nd, who wrote from his hospital bed at Fitzsimmons General Hospital in Denver. "Time will dim but never entirely erase the memory of our trying experiences." He echoed his executive officer's summary of the battle, namely being hopelessly surrounded. "Surrender," he wrote, "seemed to be the only solution to avoid needless loss of life and further suffering." Charles Whiting reported that for this, some members of the 422nd are said to have spat upon their colonel, refusing to look him in the eyes as they shuffled as prisoners towards Gerolstein. Some men are said to have picked the golden lion out of their shoulder patch thread by thread, as *Golden Lions*—their motto—don't surrender. Given that "there was little we could do" to further any battle operations, "the paramount question became that of saving the lives of as many of you men as possible."

A better summary of the Bulge experience might be the story Martin King told us in the woods above Foy. A survivor of the Bulge and of the brutal POW camps, he returned safely home, but could never get warm. He moved to Florida to work and eventually to retire, but even into old age wore extra socks on feet that always stayed cold. When he died, his daughter brought the undertaker her dad's clothes. She instructed him to put on extra socks. Her daddy would be cold no more.

Sherlock Holmes told Dr. Watson, "There's nothing more deceptive than an obvious fact." And the obvious fact was that I'd never know. There were too many men with a million overlapping stories; Dad had too scant a memory; I had way too little to go on. I could not accurately trace Dad's passage from Glasgow to St. Vith, to say nothing of the internal landscape I got only glimpses of.

My thoughts were circling, circling. I had *almost* halfway talked myself into hoping that a great curtain would open at some point on this nearly completed journey, that I would somehow pierce the cloud of unknowing, and revelation would burst through like a shaft of silver-white light. Perhaps I even believed the River Clyde had polished to a shine some holy grail. All that was hidden would emerge with just one tremulous sip.

But even if I could see the past, I'd never be able to give back to Dad all that he had lost trudging those one thousand miles from the autumn into the winter of 1944, from Glasgow to those Belgian woods. I'd never be able to liberate him from his war and POW memories.

Wilfred Owen wrote about the damage of the great guns in WWI.[48] I can only hope, and I do reasonably believe, that it turned out for Dad the way Owen hoped it would for all battle survivors. Of the terrible guns, he wrote:

But when thy spell be cast complete and whole
May God curse thee, and cut thee from our soul.

Dad may have purged the war from his system. He may have forgotten, or made some inner peace, or a deal. Either he may have excised the horrors from his soul, or God had done it for him. I'd never know. I did know that he never once complained about the war. He never once used the war as an excuse or a reason to cut to the front of the line. And as much as I wanted to know how it motivated or haunted him, I never, ever would.

Sons have a way of wanting impossible things from their fathers.

It is not uncommon for pilgrims to carry with them something from home to be left behind at the end of their journey. Quite unexpectedly this concrete seawall appeared to be a solid, definite end, but I had brought nothing from home to leave behind, nothing to throw into the Clyde, no ashes, no hand written poem, no symbolic object. I didn't have a photograph of my soldier father to tear up and release into the current of steel colored waves. Nothing. I jammed my empty hands into the front pockets of my jeans. I had an Oyster Card, two room keys to our London apartment at the Cloisters, a camera, a handful of coins, a few fibers of lint but no offering worthy of this unexpected moment. Nothing to give up. Nothing to leave behind at this altar. Despite my having planned so well, it astonished me that I had come so far and reached this moment so ill prepared, so empty-handed.

Keeping the pace of a typical teenager, the boys should have dragged Rachel all the way back to Buchanan Street by now. I knew I needed to leave this river. I needed to let go of this cold metal handrail, let go of my disappointment, and catch up. It was chilly. The walk back would warm me up. I didn't want to miss the buying spree downtown. I didn't want to miss my own sons growing up.

But I needed just one more minute. There were a few more things I needed to look at before I put them away. If I could, there were just a few things I wanted to say to my father, beginning with, *"I hope you have forgiven me for badgering you all those years."*

The silver-gray water whipped into whitecaps. Clouds had settled lower, thicker. On Buchanan they sell tartan scarves, tweed jackets, and woolen, cable sweaters. My thin, blue sweatshirt barely did the trick. But I was not shivering because of the cold.

I didn't want to leave. I could use another minute, one more day. But it was time. It was time for me to join my family.

And it was also time for me to forgive Dad for his silence. If it is true that as much meaning can reside in absence as in presence—as suggested by a painter's use of negative space—in this regard, Dad's silence was unintentional gift. In talking about the war, Bill Matthews was a man of few words. When I was a child he told me what he thought I could handle. By the time I was grown he had told me everything he had the power to say. There are limits to what human memory can hold and what the heart can express. He told me what he could. That would have to be good enough.

It is, Dad. It is.

17

Going, Going, Gone

Roy Blount, Jr. suggests two of the greatest two-word sentences are "Jesus wept" and "Go figure." Another of his best is my favorite: "I'm home."

On our first night back in the States, after everyone else had gone to bed, I petted the dog, made friends again with the cat, showered, and checked the door locks. At 4 a.m. London time I eased into my side of our bed vaguely aware that not every man who needed rest that night would get it, and certainly not everyone had a bed as soft as mine or a wife as lovely.

I heard my father's voice. *Pardon our sins, O Lord, and make us truly grateful . . .*

And then—

My bed is a boat. And I am floating on a river. The Clyde? The upper part of the James as it meanders through pastures below Bremo Bluff near Fork Union? No, I smell salt and mud. I am on tidal water. I smell field onions rising from a fresh-cut lawn. It is hot. I taste Mom's sweet tea on my lips. I hear voices, laughter, distant music. I am floating.

I am falling quickly to sleep, blinking heavily. He is stepping toward me, coming into soft focus. This is him with grey hair before it went completely white. He is older than all my friends' fathers, but still thin, still able. This is him before COPD announced each breath with a wheeze. And we are at Fort Monroe at the Thursday night summer band concert. We are on the grass near the wide steps of the Chamberlain Hotel. I smell the Chesapeake Bay. Scouts are selling hotdogs. Children are turning cartwheels in the field.

Our bodies are stuck in the present, but thankfully our minds are not. Most of us surf in and out of the present and the past, back and forth. There are no clear lines between *is* and *was* in the waters of the human mind.

The anomalies of memory are such that past and present sometimes align so precisely we have to step back to see which is which. And sometimes we catch a wave of such enormous height, we see the future, or think we see it, shining brightly in the hills and sky above the beach. Some of our boys may have caught such a glimpse when the ramps thudded open on the beaches of Normandy, and salt, blood, water, and steel caught them full in their young faces.

Time—for some—may rob the past of its power to do harm. Pain fades, Pierre-Auguste Renoir said, but the beauty remains. I hope that was true for my father and for all of the others. But memory can remain vivid. And even the distance of decades doesn't stop our hearts from pounding.

I myself am slipping off into a dream, a dream of a *memory*. My boat rides high upon the smooth muscles of water.

I've asked him to come with me to the seawall. We leave Mom at our spot on the lawn and are walking through the crowd, around the psychedelic edges of colored picnic blankets, excusing ourselves over the rows and rows of bare feet belonging to the crowd of happy spectators, countless fractal patterns of easy people limbered by dinner and summer heat and music from the bandstand. I can't remember if I am holding his hand or not, but I feel the first hints of evening cool on my sunburned neck. As we get closer to the seawall, I hear dark waves rushing louder and louder over rocks slick with green. I am excited we are together, that I have my dad all to myself.

Every detail is clear, a purer, cleaner vision. Is this what the past becomes without the clutter of wakefulness, when the demands of cognition begin to fray, or are let go of? This is why some people fear their dreams, and should.

But I do not.

I am eleven-years-old. This wilting, muggy night makes everything run in slow motion. It is steamy even with a stronger-than-usual breeze from the bay. The sun has long-set behind the distant Newport News Point, melting into the big shipyard cranes. Grabbing hold at the corner of the sky, the sun has yanked down the reds and hot oranges with it, leaving a reluctant line of violet and blue simmering on the western horizon. To our east, the bay is green and cool and endless.

I have pestered Dad to join me at the wide seawall for a foot race. I have been practicing my sprint alone, now I want to test it out on a victim.

"I'm not going to race you," he insists as we stroll through the crowd.

I say the word "race," and he swats me away like an insect. I know he will not race. He is ancient, fifty-one years old. Certainly he is molasses slow, but I am bugging him anyway.

"Why not?" I say, in my best daring voice. I beg. I have actually never before seen my dad run, but I assume he can do it. And I'll be a good sport and take it easy on him.

"I'm not going to race you," he keeps saying as he walks me through the maze of blankets and folding chairs spread out on the ample grounds around the bandstand. The crowd claps and sings along. Some adults slow dance at the edge of their blankets. Sweaty little kids, exhausted from running around, sleep in their parent's strong arms. The kids who are awake dance and gyrate and play duck-duck-goose with parents mellow from wine and fried chicken, from too perfect a night.

The Army Continental Band cooks. The bandstand shines like a snow-white moth suspended in an inky sky on tremendous, elegant wings. Horns blare. The drummer is in another world. The conductor moves like the music has gotten into his blood stream. The band plays with their eyes squeezed shut, blowing the notes out so furiously that it seems their heads might pop. For their part, the notes are clamoring out of the instruments. Every player is soaking wet, feverishly glowing under that ring of white-hot spotlights. The bandstand hovers above the dark green grass like a mirage.

Other dads pace on the wide seawall with their antsy, bored kids. The harbor opens into the bay, its gentler waters mingling with ones wild from their passage across the lower bay from the darker-still ocean. Ships are making their way one by one into the awaiting arms of unseen marine terminals and piers. Not far from us is the Strawberry Banks that the first English settlers hungrily fell upon. I keep asking Dad to race me down that wide seawall. He keeps saying no.

Why, Dad? Why?

He is unmoved. I am not consoled.

Please, Dad, please.

My mom and hundreds of others relax on picnic blankets on the grass. They applaud with an energy that the heat would not have allowed if it weren't for the power of the music. I walk circles around Dad asking him please, please, please to race me. We walk, but I want to run. I want to run, run, run. I want to show off my speed. Every boy wants to make his dad proud. And every boy wants to best his old man. Naturally, I want Dad to eat my dust.

When the band counts down into their second or third encore medley, without warning, Dad catapults down that seawall. Nothing in my small head leads me to predict this. I am stunned. It takes a few seconds to realize I am getting what I had asked for. I am getting a race, and I better start running or he'll end up two miles away at Dog Beach before I take a single step.

I charge after him. And I pour it on. Despite my fearsome speed, the distance between my dad and me widens. I lean into it. But he is drawing away from me still. The click, click, clicking of his street shoes pops like gunfire. How can this be? He is running like the bionic man. I churn my legs faster and faster but it still isn't enough. It isn't close to being near enough.

My eyes go wide as the soles of his J.C. Penny shoes amazingly spark the concrete. The seawall cracks then shatters beneath his pounding legs. Showers of powdery stone rise first, then, out of the cloud, the blazing stripes of flame. He runs so fast it creates a great wind. Waves jump the seawall, trees whip back and forth, endangered ships sound alarms and drop anchor. The band holds the crowd's attention like a black hole folding all matter into itself; they are riveted to the players transfiguring to light on the bandstand. Nobody but spy satellites notices the melting path my dad is leaving behind.

I watch him get smaller and smaller, a dot at the end of the seawall racing for the redoubts and gun emplacements once maintained by a lieutenant-engineer from West Point named Robert E. Lee before he became a confederate turncoat. *Look away, Dixie, look away.*

Dad is flat gone, and I am breathless, awed. I stand alone on the shore of the whole wide world. All I can do is jog awkwardly behind. All I can do is watch my dad disappear.

Selected Notes

Chapter 2/Gently Back to Earth

1 RAMP, Recovered Allied Military Personnel, (retrieved March 16, 2013): www.med-dept.com/ramps.php

2 The Cigarette Camps: The US Army Camps in the Le Havre Area. The remembrances of Red Cross nurse Josephine Bovill, (retrieved July 12, 2011): www.skylighters.org/special/cigcamps/cmplstrk.html

3 www.nerdworld.com/cgi-bin/jump.cgi?7096 and www.mm.com/user/jpk are dead websites retrieved May 15, 2011, comprised of the writings of Sgt. John Kline (M company, 423rd regiment); Kline was dug in just south of my father. His war journals can be found by searching the Indianamilitary.org site.

4 (Retrieved June 2011): John Kline, www.indianamilitary.org/106ID/SoThinkMenu/106thSTART.htm. From entries on 1/13/45 and 3/21/45. (See note number three.)

5 Thomas Saylor, *Long Hard Road: American POWs During World War II* (Minnesota Historical Society Press, 1st edition, November 15, 2007).

Chapter 3/Blood and Guts

6 Tony Vercoe, *Survival at Stalag IVB: Soldier and Airmen Remember Germany's Largest POW Camp of World War II* (London: MacFarland and Company, 2006), 32, from the official record of the Food Providing Ministry, published top secret, Berlin 24-11-1941, and the director in Ministry Herr Mansfeld and Herr Moritz.

7 Michael M. Phillips, *The Lobotomy Files*, Wall Street Journal. Series available online at WSJ, (retrieved October 2015) projects.wsj.com/lobotomyfiles/?ch=one&mg=inert-wsj

Chapter 4/Midnight Is A Place

8 A History of PTSD, a useful website created by Kasey P.S. Goodpaster, doctoral candidate, counseling psychology, Purdue University. See (retrieved October 2015): historyofptsd.wordpress.com/post-wwii-and-vietnam/

9 Easy Company, 2nd Battalion of the 506th Parachute Infantry Regiment of the 101st Airborne Division.

10 Casualty reports vary. See US Department of Defense.

11 Hugh Marshall Cole, *Ardennes: The Battle of the Bulge*, from the US Army in WWII series, (Office of the Chief of Military History, US Army, 1964), xiii.

12 George MacDonald Fraser, *Quartered Safe Out Here: A Harrowing Tale of World War II*, (New York: Skyhorse Publishing, 2007), xii.

13 Joe Hilbers, *Battle of the Bulge: One Private's Story*, available on Hilbers' website (retrieved May 2011): www.vittlesvoyages.com/

14 Charles Whiting, *Death of a Division*, (New York: Stein and Day, 1981), 35.

15 Hugh Marshall Cole, *Ardennes: The Battle of the Bulge*, from the US Army in WWII series, (Office of the Chief of Military History, US Army, 1964), 146.

16 Hugh Marshall Cole, *Ardennes: The Battle of the Bulge*, from the US Army in WWII series, (Office of the Chief of Military History, US Army, 1964), 166.

17 Hugh Marshall Cole, *Ardennes: The Battle of the Bulge*, from the US Army in WWII series, (Office of the Chief of Military History, US Army, 1964), 165.

18 Robert Frost, *Desert Places*.

19 Bud Street's unpublished journal, from the library of Calder and Glenda Ehrmann.

20 Hugh Marshall Cole, *Ardennes: The Battle of the Bulge*, from the US Army in WWII series, (Office of the Chief of Military History, US Army, 1964), 170.

21 For one list of WWII massacres, see George Duncan's webpage (retrieved October 2015): //members.linet.net.au/~gduncan/massacres

22 Richard Chess, "Holocaust Day" from *Tekiah*, (University of Georgia Press: 1994).

Chapter 7/The 9:49 to Paris-Nord

23 Charles Whiting, *Death of a Division*, (New York: Stein and Day, 1981).

Chapter 8/Luminous Paris

24 Ernie Pyle, *Brave Men*, (Lincoln: University of Nebraska Press, 2001), 483-484.

25 David McCullough, *The Greater Journey: Americans in Paris*, (New York: Simon and Schuster, 2011), 23.

26 Ernie Pyle, *Brave Men*, (Lincoln: University of Nebraska Press, 2001), 324, 490.

Chapter 9/Normandy

27 Bill Bryson, *Neither Here nor There: Travels in Europe*. (New York: Perinnial, 2001), 68.

28 Associated Press, obituary of Edith Shain, June 24, 2010.

Chapter 10/A Perfect View

29 William Watson, *Paris Universal Exposition: Civil Engineering, Public Works, and Architecture* (Washington: Government Printing office, 1892), 833.

30 John Pimlott, *Battle of the Bulge*, (London: Bison Books Limited, 1981), 33.

Chapter 11/Neither Sighing

31 "Medical Bulletin No. 1", dated May 15, 1945. See (retrieved March 16, 2013): http://med-dept.com/ramps.php

32 Lyon G. Tyler, *History of Hampton and Elizabeth City County Virginia* (Hampton, VA: The Board of Supervisors of Elizabeth City County, Hampton, Virginia, 1922), 16.

33 Lyon G. Tyler, *History of Hampton and Elizabeth City County Virginia* (Hampton, VA: The Board of Supervisors of Elizabeth City County, Hampton, Virginia, 1922), 13.

Chapter 12/Making Full Use of the Platform and Minding the Gap

34 Joseph Littell, *A Lifetime In Every Moment: A Memoir* (New York: Houghton Mifflin Company, 1995), 158.

35 Roscoe C. Blunt, Jr, *Foot Soldier: A Combat Infantryman's War in Europe* (Cambridge, Mass: Da Capo Press, 2002), 124.

36 See the US Census Bureau. (retrieved June 2011): http://www.census.gov/prod/www/statistical-abstract-03.html

37 Reproduced from the original typescript, War Department, Washington DC; 3rd edition, 2005 from the Bodleian Library, University of Oxford.

Chapter 13/A Riddle of Steel and Stone

38 Tate Modern's wall plaque, *Sleeping Venus*. June 2011.

39 Jack Rogers, *Presbyterian Creeds: A Guide to the Book of Confessions*, (Louisville: Westminster John Knox Press, 1985), 182.

40 *Book of Confessions*, (Presbyterian Church, USA, the Office of the General Assembly, 100 Witherspoon Street, Louisville, KY, 2002), 246.

41 *Instructions for American Servicemen in Britain, 1942*. The "Britain At War" segment. (pages unnumbered.)

Chapter 15/Bridge Over Troubled Water

42 Mark Chirnside, *RMS Aquitania: The Ship Beautiful*, (Stroud, Gloucestershire: The History Press, 2008), 89.

43 Robert Lightbody has a great website about the Aquitania and other ocean liners. He lives in the West End of Glasgow. (Retrieved May 2011): www.roblightbody.com/liners/aquitania/emails.htm

44 A letter from Larry Moler about his father, Jimmie, to Robert Lightbody, (retrieved July 2011): www.roblightbody.com/liners/aquitania/emails.htm

45 Joseph Littell, *A Lifetime In Every Moment: A Memoir* (New York: Houghton Mifflin Company, 1995), 112.

46 Kenneth H. Grant's unpublished war journal. IndianiaMilitary. org has a great collection of these journals. For Grant's, see (retrieved October 2015): www.indianamilitary.org/german%20PW%20Camps/ Prisoner%20of%20War/PW%20Camps/Stalag%20IV-B%20Mulberg/ KennethHGrant/KennethGrant

47 From a letter home by Rae Marlin Litaker, July 14, 1943. Written on official stationary: "United States Army Air Forces 36th Street Air Base, Miami, Florida."

Chapter 16/If Only I'd Listened to Sherlock Holmes

48 Wilfred Owen, *On Seeing a Piece of Our Artillery Brought into Action.*